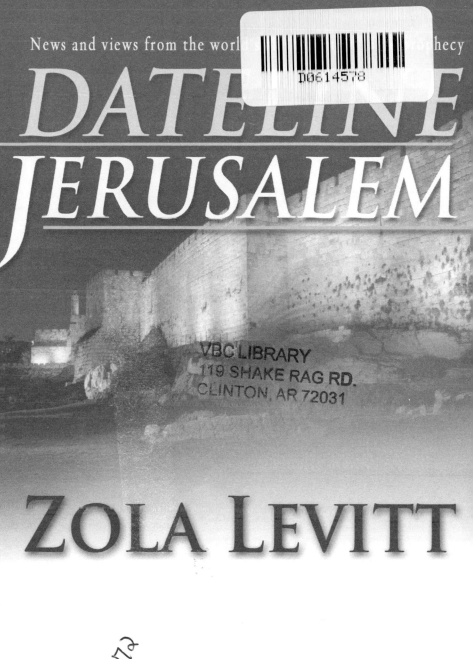

News and views from the worl... ...hecy

DATELINE JERUSALEM

ZOLA LEVITT

Balfour
Books

First printing: June 2005

ISBN: 0-89221-625-5
Library of Congress Control Number: 2005925566

Cover by Brent Spurlock

Unless otherwise noted, all Scripture is from the King James Version of the Bible.

Printed in the United States of America

Please visit our website for other great titles:
www.balfourbooks.net

For information regarding author interviews,
please contact the publicity department at (870) 438-5288.

ACKNOWLEDGMENTS

Authors usually acknowledge extraordinary help on the part of manuscript editors, etc., but I want to say that I have a real appreciation for our ministry employees who gave wonderful assistance in gathering all the various elements that make up this particular book. I am fortunate to have such help and always conscious of the fact that in our ministry all workers are equal before the Lord, including yours truly. To God, soldiers at the rear of any army are as important as the field marshal, which He demonstrated many times.

I'm just glad to be a soldier in His army.

Special thanks to Beth Mull, Alan Himber, and Cynthia Smith, and for the invaluable and ongoing help of my son Mark, business manager of Zola Levitt Ministry. And above all, the Lord and the wife He provided me are responsible for the thoughts in this book.

Contents

ZOLA'S TESTIMONY —
HOW IT ALL
STARTED

As I reported in one of my early books, "I was dragged kicking and screaming to Christ by Gentiles."

I've simplified my testimony these days down to the fact that I was the most ordinary individual to witness to. I was not a drunk. I was not into drugs. I was not desperate about most anything. The only problem was that like Jesus, Peter, Paul, and all of the Bible writers, Old Testament and New, I was Jewish.

Thus, it wasn't until my 32nd year that Christian people at last indicated to me that the Messiah had come. I'm glad they did that. In the ensuing time, I have spoken to around 100 million people about Christ.

A friend named Dan, whom I had known most of my life, asked me a question which became one of my book titles. He wrote and inquired "How did a fat, balding, middle-age Jew like you become a Jesus freak?" That was in 1972, and I answered him to the best of my ability with a whole book on that subject. Toward the end of it, he sent me a letter saying, "I asked. He answered. I believe." So that testimony worked out fine.

I won't go into all the details that we discussed, but since I'm writing my testimony here, I will quote from the first and second letters:

Dear Dan:

In Louisville, in 1971, I attended my first church service in my life. I had been tangling with Campus Crusaders, who witnessed to me at the beginning, and they advised me to read the Book of John. I was told I could buy a New Testament at the home of the campus director, and so I did that. I went by night like Nicodemus and bought a New Testament bound by it-self, what Dr. Thomas S. McCall, senior theologian of our ministry and expert in the Old Testament, refers to as the "The Amputated Bible." I was really going to read with the purpose of refuting the arguments that my testifiers kept throwing at me.

I sat down with the Book of John, more to find ways to criticize Christ than to learn the gospel. But that was impossible. "Which of you convicts me of sin?" the Lord asks in John. I had no answers. What a man!

A friend took me to her church in Louisville one weekend. I verbally assaulted the preacher after the service. He had moved me — but good — when he called for souls to receive Christ, and I went up after the service just to blast him intellectually. But it came out the same as with my friend. He was a polite listener and a compassionate person. His mind was clear and he met my arguments head-on. I was the one who got blasted.

That night, March 14, 1971, I received Christ. I said, "If you're there, show me."

Dan, I can't share with you, close as we have always been, just what that moment and all subsequent events in my life have been like. I won't try to tell you some yarn about my being sinless. You know me better than that. Suffice it to say He showed me.

Zola

My friend wrote back immediately, saying, "Tell me *how* He showed you," and I replied:

Dear Dan:

I've prayed for guidance to be able to answer your searching question. My first feeling is that unless you can crawl into my head and my heart, you'll never understand this and I'll never be able to get it across.

My first big moment, besides my friend's perfect witness, was John 1:45–51. I wasn't much of a
Crucifixion-Resurrection man back then, but I was
wholly delighted to see that Jesus Christ had a sense of
humor. "You like fig tree tricks, do you? Well, let me
tell you something, buddy. . . ."

I remember looking up over the Bible and thinking, *He's cool. I wish I'd said that.*

Then there was His likable stubbornness. I'm no
"gentle Jesus, meek and mild" man either, and I don't
know where they get that stuff. I could really get with
His wild-eyed self-confidence, though. Check John
3:3. Nicodemus comes up and sort of says, "Look,
teacher, I've got some smarts, too. And I wanted to
discuss. . . ." And right there the Lord cuts him off
and says, in effect, "You haven't been born yet, mister."
There are subtle levels of meaning to this retort, but I
was delighted on the novice level.

And John 14:6! What kind of madman says, "I am
the way and the truth and the life. Nobody gets to the
Father except by me"? I mean, He's either who He says
He is or He needs a shrink. No use patronizing Him,
I read somewhere, by calling Him a great moralist or
humanitarian. Not "the way, the truth, and the life."

I could see as a writer that the stuff I was reading
was no mere fabrication. The content and the style
are too mismatched. It's so-so reportage, leaving lots
of gaps. But the meanings! Let's say, no writer that

bad could write so good. If a guy capable of inventing John 14:6 made the whole thing up, the story would have been polished to a high perfection. As it is, some of the writing is badly disjointed, scenes aren't set adequately, and there's a lot of reportage that doesn't follow the party line. (Why would a fabricator put in Peter's denial?)

But all that is what reached me out of the gospel. You might not feel the same way at all. A better answer to your question would involve what went on in my life.

Take the time my English horn was stolen. I came home one day, back in Bloomington, to find my house ransacked and my English horn gone. You may remember something about that horn. I don't know if I had told you its history — the miracle of finding it in a pawn shop on Third Avenue in New York City, repairing it lovingly, and performing on it for several years. What a horn! But the maker died decades ago, and it was irreplaceable. It took almost daily adjustments to keep the ancient machine parts going, and very special reeds to stay in tune on that worn bore.

(I was just thinking that I owe my whole relationship with that fine old horn to your influence back in high school. You were the one who got me playing oboe.)

Anyway, it was gone. And I found burned books of matches all around the house, thrown on the floors and under the beds. Apparently, the thief had tried to burn my house down. He had left my oboe, an instrument much easier to resell, and had taken the horn from right beside it. *How dumb he was*, I thought.

And here goes the part I was telling you about — I could think of nothing but how pathetically confused that robber must have been. Maybe he was a head case or a drunk. I prayed for him with all the earnestness I had in me. Nothing else occurred to me to do at the time. I asked God to reach this muddle-headed thief and straighten him out. I honestly tell you — buddy's honor — I forgot about the horn. I really haven't thought about it since.

Something about having Christ makes you wise and spontaneous about life. You are able to see the inside core of things. Like He did when He dealt with the sinners He forgave. You gain a respect for things human and a detachment from things temporal.

There's also a sensation of a conflict within. Sin becomes, for the first time, in my case, a real issue. My behavior became very important to me. Not to impress the next guy, or to provide "a good witness for the Lord," but to have the kind of peace that I discovered the moment I received Christ. My huge ego began to slip away at that instant. The process is still continuing — I never realized just how huge it was! But as I let the Lord take over the inner province inch by inch, my life makes better and better sense, and I am more and more knowledgeable about who I am and what I'm here for.

And the reaction to other people undergoes a very dramatic change. Increasingly, I became more aware of people's motives for talking or acting the way they did, rather than just reacting to the action. This feels to me like a first step in learning to love all people — a pretty good trick, but one that Jesus commanded.

These are things, just off the top of my head, that He "showed me" and is continuing to show me. I could go on and on, but we would get into subtleties that would truly be difficult to communicate in common terms. I'm not trying to "cop out," but just say that the Lord helps Zola with Zola's things, not Dan's, and I'm not sure the whole message is transferable.

Prayer is another thing I should mention. The Lord promised that we believers will have whatever we want. "Anything you ask, believing. . . ." The final word there is a big one. But I've prayed away an abscessed tooth, poverty, sex problems, and even moods that were bothering me. I can also reliably give my worries and cares over to Him and see them comfortably resolved. There's more to say about this area.

Lastly, you are witness to the fact that a wandering ne'er-do-well can become a published author in no time at all, with the help of God. See Romans 8:28. At this point of my life, I have no job, but am seeing the Lord provide completely. I have no doubt whatsoever that He will guide me "in the way thou shalt take" so that my life will be, as he promised, "abundant."

As for "that moment" when I received Christ, it was thunderous for me, although I understand everyone does not experience an emotional sensation. I had a tremendous feeling of well-being that pervaded the next few days, as if I were on some kind of high. The euphoria eased, or perhaps I grew accustomed to it. But I can say that that moment marked the beginning of a period of zero depression for me. Since that moment, I have been impatient, angry, and discouraged, and lots of common earthly negative feelings have been with me as always. But I have not been depressed. I have not for a moment felt out of control of myself, wallowing in sadness. This was previously common for me.

My self-esteem is a new feeling, since I am "a new creature." I do all things in Christ "who strengthens me."

I hope this clears things up a bit. Your turn.

Zola

I'm sorry that the book has gone out of print over the past 30 years or so, but there are many like it. When a believer testifies to an unbeliever honest enough to ask questions and get into a debate, a powerful thing happens. The Holy Spirit seems to draw the witnessee to the Lord, and I've seen it throughout my ministry. All Christians who have witnessed are aware of this small miracle which has so eternal an effect.

It was incidents like this that seemed to call me to reach out as far as I could with a witness. I quit a good job to go to Campus Crusade, and to witness as far and wide as my talents would allow me. I asked the Lord to make me a good witness.

Right from the beginning, God seemed to lead me and to prosper whatever I attempted. I was impressed to write books almost as soon as I was saved — even though I had never done that before. I did not seek work after the end of my year working with Campus Crusade, but rather sat home typing all day. My last day of work with Campus Crusade was in 1972, and I have not had an outside job since then.

Early on when I was book-writing, I came to an impasse. I did not have my month's rent and it was already the third. In the apartment complex where I lived, people were curious as to why I was home all day, sometimes by the pool, and always available. Was I independently wealthy? Was I a night watchman somewhere? Or was I simply a bum? Well, I had told one and all that I worked for the Lord and did not have to report somewhere on a daily basis, but only had to write.

But now I was faced with having to go into the offices of the apartment complex and beg not to be evicted because I didn't have my rent. I went out on the patio where I could see plenty of sky, and remonstrated with God, saying, "It's all very fine for You to say 'Consider the lilies of the field' and 'the birds of the air,' but I don't have my rent. What am I supposed to say to these people? What kind of representative am I of faith when I cannot meet a necessary expense, and yet I have testified that You are my rock and my support?"

After that half-hour of telling off the Lord, I went downstairs and checked the mail. All the while I had been on the patio, a check for $500, more than double the rent needed, was waiting in the mailbox. It was the advance for a book I had sent to Moody Press months before and had almost forgotten. I still have that check dated August 3, 1972, in a glass frame.

The Lord had me continue writing books for some 20 years until I had published fully 40 of them with outside publishers and another 10 or 12 through our own ministry. They were all good sellers. My average was some 60,000 copies per title after I had written quite a few books, and publishers of all sorts were after me. I started with prophecy in Israel, but branched out into writing about everything under the sun — dieting, exercise, etc. — but always with a Christian publisher and always honoring the Lord. It came to a point where publishers would call me and ask what I'd been thinking about lately and would I like to write about that for them. The Lord was really a blessing in that ministry.

To make a long story short, I wrote some books that sold pretty well, and I was living on those royalties when I undertook a radio talk show. My radio program, too, prospered very well. It beat a secular talk show on a 50,000-watt open channel station in the most important market. There was a time when people would stop their cars and go to a pay phone booth to call the program. I really think I learned more Bible from those people who called my radio talk show than from many seminary professors. I was contacted by the local CBN-affiliated television station. They wanted me to buy airtime. They pointed out that I had a built-in audience from the radio and that those people would support this new local outreach.

And they exclaimed, "We love you, Zola."

I asked, "But how *much* do you love me?"

The television program started slowly and I was very nervous about it, since I paid for everything out of my earlier book royalties. It was costing four figures per week to make a local program that brought back five or ten letters at a time. Some of them had $1.00, some of them just thanks and congratulations. The folks at the post office where I had chosen the largest available P.O. box gave me baleful looks as I called for my pitiful few donations every week.

Then Virginia Beach called. It seemed that the national Christian Broadcasting Network program director developed a curiosity about "a Jewish guy preaching the gospel," and wanted to see a tape. I flew to Virginia Beach with the Passover tape in my hand and urged the program director that this material needed to be taught. It was not in the seminaries. It was not in the churches. But it was crucial to Christian understanding. He said that we might pray about it overnight and see what God would have us do.

You really remember how to pray at a time like that. I spent the night in "much prayer," as they say, and the next morning the program director said he would try it on a national basis and see how the response was.

Well, my large-size post office box was justified. Folks everywhere responded well to the program and, like a dive bomber that almost hit the ground, the program pulled out of its doldrums just before bankruptcy. Although I had lost two-thirds of my net worth, I had stumbled after the Lord's leading and He did not fail me. As with book-writing, He came through when needed most, and my lonely ministry, with no real paychecks, went on.

At the beginning of the '80s, I seriously undertook tours of Israel with our own agency, Travel Experience International. I had visited the Holy Land on several previous tours, but these were our own, with our peculiar itinerary, which has been a great success. To date, I've taken more than 80 tours of the Holy Land, and in addition resided there for various periods of time.

In the '80s, I also began to compose and record songs that were used on the TV program, as the Lord provided them. To date, we've made some 20 albums containing over two hundred spiritual songs, and they too, it seems, have been well received. All things considered, the Lord has been more than good to me and, again, prospered all I've undertaken.

We at first hired musicians, even expanding to a full orchestra, and recorded in a professional studio in Nashville, and several times in Dallas. When synthesizers were perfected, we utilized those with instrumental overlays, but, in any case, we always produced the best quality. And, while I don't think we've really made much money on music, people love it and the Lord dictated it to me. I truly think of myself as a musical stenographer. I had gone through a music school and hold a master's degree in that subject, along with all the course work for the doctorate, so I knew what I was doing technically. But until I started to compose for the Lord, the work was pedantic and ordinary and no one much liked it.

As an oboist, I played in the New Orleans Symphony and San Antonio Symphony, and also with the Glen Campbell Show tours when they passed through the Midwest. (I was at Indiana University at the time for my graduate music school work.) I still play the oboe, English horn, recorder, and piano for the albums featured on our programs, and in certain ones, like *The First Christians*, I composed the pieces for prominent oboe solos and I play those solos myself.

During the '80s and '90s, we also expanded the ministry newsletter into a virtual 32-page magazine with color pictures, and it too has been quite popular. It certainly helps to raise funds for the TV outreach, something I've never had a taste for doing.

I'm appalled by what goes on in Christian television, truth to tell. There are many programs where fundraising is pretty much the only activity, and I can't fathom why people give their money to such organizations. To have a ministry that you can bring to supporters and to ask that it be financed makes perfect sense. But to simply demand money without demonstrating any ministry at all or because God is supposed to return more than you gave somehow, doesn't seem to be up to biblical standards in my mind.

I'm often asked about Christian giving, which is voluntary and a privilege and not limited to the Old Covenant tithe of ten percent. But typically the question takes the form of, "If I give to God, does He have to return one-and-a-half times what I've given, as I was told by some teacher?" My answer is always the same. I tell them that I only speak on giving. They are asking me about investing and they need to ask an investment counselor.

Where money is concerned, I just don't covet it, and despite all my sins, taking donations to enrich myself is not one of them. Truly, I thank God that I don't have luxurious tastes. He has made me comfortable and kept me working for Him, and that's all I really have ever wanted. I'm not trying to criticize anyone else, and I have my own excesses, but money is a topic that comes up all the time in religious broadcasting, and I resent being lumped in with those who make it a priority in their ministries. Zola Levitt Ministries spends about one-half of one percent of its time raising funds, and that has proved to be enough. As the Scripture says, we make our needs known and we leave the rest to the Lord. He's always come through for us.

So, in sum, my testimony adds up to the fact that God sent willing Christians after a very ordinary Jewish man and made him into a unique talent and employed him for 34 years and counting. I haven't mentioned my family or my personal life, but those are in good order, and I want my testimony to focus mainly on the work the Lord has me doing.

I was given some kind of remarkable set of gifts, totally unpredictably, when I was saved. Think about it. I had never

written a book. I had never written a spiritual song. I had
never gone to Israel. I had never been even vaguely interested
in Christianity, to say nothing of Judaism. I was not particularly a godly individual. I did have a thorough Jewish education, consisting of seven years in Hebrew school and ten years
in Sunday School. I was Bar Mitzvahed and confirmed. I
stayed around the synagogue after my Bar Mitzvah (as many
do not) and sang in the choir. I eventually became the conduc-
tor of the young people's choir and served in that capacity for
some time.

But I was always hungry again.

Now I'm completely full.

Chapter Two

THE JEWS —
A BLESSING UNTO
ALL NATIONS

B ack when I was in college, I read a book by E.B. White, who wrote chapters on different subjects he had experienced in his long and interesting career. He was a secular intellectual, and he simply looked at the world around him and took up various topics willy-nilly, as he pleased. He knew something on each one and I found the book very interesting. It is the inspiration for this book.

One of E.B. White's chapters was simply called "The Jews," and he said quite a bit about them. He appreciated the fact that the Jews are truly a phenomenon in this world. "And I will make of thee a great nation . . . and in thee shall all families of the earth be blessed" (Gen. 12:2–3).

In my own affairs, I've gone to Israel so repeatedly over my Christian lifetime that I know quite a bit about what's happening there on all sides of the "controversy" over land ownership. I put the term controversy in quotation marks because there's no real controversy going on over there at all. It's completely phony that there is "strife," "danger," "a crisis," "a war," etc. These are all media dramatizations of the normal course of events in any democracy dealing with terrorists, including the United States.

I always cite the case of our State Department, which is inevitably quick to criticize Israel. It publishes "travel warnings" about visiting Jerusalem. I realize that Washington, where its offices are located, and Jerusalem are the same size, both having a population of around 700,000 in the corporate limits. Just for fun, I looked up the statistics in one of the years where it published those warnings and found that 25 people had been killed in Jerusalem in various terrorist activities, and 233 were killed in Washington in ordinary street shootings. Well, since Washington was almost ten times more dangerous than Israel, I was naturally curious where the travel warnings were for Washington. And why not an international peace conference for Washington? How about an Oslo agreement? How about something to protect the people who might try to visit there?

All that is tongue-in-cheek, of course, but I have no idea to this day why we portray Israel as a very dangerous nation. Obviously, it gets one's attention that buses have been blown up and terrorists have attacked schools and all the rest of that.

People are indeed killed there by the Palestinians. But murders happen in the United States, too, and on a greater scale. Israel does not have shootings in post offices or gang fights and murders in families, and has nothing at all like the street violence, drug deals, Mafia activity, and so on that is common in the United States. In fact, in Israel there are very few crimes against persons. A burglar would be fortunate if the police got to him before the neighbors did.

And all that is not to mention Oklahoma City, the Pentagon attack, and the unparalleled World Trade Center terrorism.

Israel is, after all, "one *mishpocha*." That is, a family. They are all descendants of Abraham, and within a family, and while there's a certain amount of strife, the people don't usually kill each other. Considering those statistics of ordinary killings among the American population, the terrorism in Israel actually turns out quite puny in comparison to the United States.

Almost any democracy has violence, because in a democracy the poor people can come out and express themselves, and sometimes they overdo it. But the issue in Israel again is just a phony. The Palestinians have no real reason to hate the Israelis, nor do any other Arabs. In fact, if the Arabs were to accept the Israelis as the good neighbors they are and the true holders of a land given to them 4,000 years ago, everyone would be better off. As one sage said it, "With Arab cash and Jewish brains, the Middle East could be paradise."

But the Arabs won't have it that way. They pretend to hate Judaism. They pretend to hate democracy. They pretend to hate the United States. And it's really all about their own ineptitude. They are envious of people who get ahead of them, and the sad fact is that almost everyone in the world is ahead of them. They are primitive, backward, and cultic in their faith. The awful Wahhabism purveyed out of Saudi Arabia and taught everywhere in the world (certainly including the United States, where we welcome these maniacs) promotes the murder of innocents and all sorts of other crimes. In democracies, these crimes can flourish, and so western Europe is being overwhelmed by radical Muslims, and the United States will probably fall next.

That is not because of anything the United States has done, other than our reaching out to minorities of all sorts. It is a step too far, however, to try to accommodate people who have attacked and killed 3,000 of our citizens on our own soil. It seems too obvious to say, but we should stop kowtowing to the Muslims and get serious about restraining their influence. That is one man's opinion. I'll say more in my chapter on their ongoing takeover of the United States.

I recently interviewed a Karaite Jew, an Orthodox Jew who holds exactly to Scripture and not to rabbinical laws and traditions, in Jerusalem. I subsequently wrote to a dear Orthodox Jewish friend of mine that the Karaite was the first Jew I'd ever met who read the Scriptures and did what they said. Christians think for some reason that Jews are "walking Bibles," or that rabbis know a great deal of Scripture, but there's no truth to that at all. The Jews are among the last to read Scripture, although they carry the Torah (the Pentateuch) around the synagogue and touch it with a prayer shawl and then kiss the shawl. But they do not read it nor do they understand what it says. They claim to, but in reality they are obeying what Bible-reading people would refer to as commentaries. That is, sages and rabbis through the ages have commented on the Scriptures as to their interpretation and application in daily life, and the people obey those commentators. Naturally, that way is madness.

The control of Judaism by the rabbis is utterly amazing. Grown men walk around in Jerusalem with skull caps on their heads (not scriptural), women dutifully separate milk and meat dishes (not scriptural), and no one celebrates the festival known as First Fruits, the Sunday after Passover (scriptural). But after all, that was the day of the Resurrection and so many Jews might have become believers in the Messiah if they knew of His fulfillment of the feast.

If Islam is a kind of "replacement theology," made to replace Judaism and Christianity, then rabbinical Judaism, the kind we are familiar with these days, is also replacement theology. The rabbis delegated an enormous amount of authority to themselves (they are not mentioned in Scripture), and created a new kind of Judaism based on rules and regulations which they themselves formulate. And the entire Jewish culture defends these ideas, though they are hardly scriptural. Covering the head, for example, is not scriptural, and neither is washing the hands before eating.

When our Lord was criticized because His disciples did not wash their hands before eating, the Jewish leaders objected that He was not following the traditions of the elders, the traditions of their fathers. "Then came to Jesus scribes and Pharisees, which were of Jerusalem, saying, Why do thy disciples transgress the tradition of the elders? for they wash not their hands when they eat bread. But he answered and said unto them, Why do ye also transgress the commandment of God by your tradition?" (Matt. 15:1–3). What He's really saying is, "Why do you follow rules that aren't even in the Law and bother other people with following them, when you don't even keep the Law yourselves?"

In my book *The Trouble With Christians, The Trouble With Jews*, I comment as follows on the Jewish condition today.

Chapter 4

Manners and Mores

Frankly, the Jews live in a wonderful community. Having lived in both the Jewish and Christian worlds in my lifetime (about 50% in each), I have to testify that the Jewish community is better. It is warmer, more friendly, more enlightened, more culturally aware, more creative. Having said all that, it is a shame to see it so unspiritual. All of the compliments I might make to Judaism are of worldly things. When all is said and done, I prefer the company of believing Christians with whatever failings they may have, because ultimately the only thing worth talking about is God and His will and His plans for the future, in the view of a believer.

Jews live by "tradition," a concept celebrated in the initial song of *Fiddler on the Roof.* They have lived a certain kind of "Jewishness" for literally thousands of years and whether they are desert nomads as they once were, European black-suited Orthodox, as some still are, or advanced nuclear scientists in the modernistic laboratories of the U.S., they do things "in the Jewish way." This Jewish style certainly includes things that would be enviable to all communities. They emphasize education, the dignity of the individual, freedom for all, solid family life, good marriages, etc., etc. The Hasidic community would like to boast of these things and, truth to tell, if they were statistically figured out, it is almost a certainty that the Jews would rank high on the list as having accomplished a wonderful social adjustment, and this while being hounded and persecuted for some two thousand years, flying from country to country, assimilating or hiding in ghettos, and finally trying to defend a pitifully small land from maniacal enemies on every border.

You have to hand it to them, the Jews are doing pretty well.

But there is a false Jewish crowd also. The emphasis on material things, the estimation of Israel as a successful geopolitical entity (rather than an act of God and a Promised Land) and perhaps an unseemly worldly shrewdness, do not agree with the scriptural picture of the holy Jew. There is a tongue-in-cheek

forgiveness for Jews caught racketeering, selling junk
bonds, or prospering by various shenanigans. These
excesses are excused with a shrug, as though the paramount concern was that a Jewish person be financially
successful rather than spiritually informed. I candidly
feel a discomfort in criticizing any of my Jewish brethren, but to discuss Jewish manners and mores fairly,
one must mention some negatives. The Jewish way is
not always the best of all ways.

Books like *Chutzpa* (which means audacity or
impertinence) by Alan Dershowitz present examples
of a kind of Jewish style that is purely materialistic and
worldly. This is American Judaism at its most assimi-
lated and its most affected and, unfortunately, its most
ungodly. Pride and the intellect of a winner like Dershowitz must surely be leavened by his public defenses
of rascals and his obvious "do anything, say anything
for the good of my client" approach.

Supposedly, Jewish people vote as some sort of bloc
favoring liberal policies and Democrats. This probably does not prove true in every election. In general,
the Jews, a highly persecuted people, have favored an
emphasis on personal freedoms and a less powerful
central government. They have also sided with other
minorities, most particularly the blacks, in many issues.
Ironically, in the age of Louis Farrakhan (leader of the
Nation of Islam), the blacks have hardly returned the
favor. Those blacks who have embraced the Nation of

Islam, or have otherwise become Muslims, seem to become anti-Jewish for no good reason. Jews, of course, were instrumental in the Civil Rights movement and typically could be found on the front lines of the earliest struggles. They still favor all possible liberties for all possible downtrodden groups, in general.

Interestingly enough, those Jews who are unspiritual are celebrated by those blacks who are Bible believers. It is well-known that Negro spirituals usually concern Old Testament stories ("Joshua Fit de Battle of Jericho," "Swing Low Sweet Chariot," "Go Down Moses," etc.). Some blacks, very conscious of their own period of slavery, side with their brothers in bonds, the Old Testament Jews. Yet other blacks, conscious of their period in slavery, accuse the contemporary Jews, with no evidence in fact, of having been slaveholders in colonial America.

The celebration of worldly accomplishment is replete in the Jewish community, and the truth is that there are many accomplished Jews to celebrate. A terrifically impressive list of actors, musicians, doctors, lawyers, scientists, etc., can be compiled, and often has been. The whole world knows that the Jews excel in the professions, and it sometimes takes exception on that very point. "The Jews own all the banks," goes the old saw, assuming that Jews are crafty and far ahead of the competition and thus control the money and ultimately cause depressions and cataclysms. This nonsense reaches its apex in conspiracy theories that hold that the Jews are taking over the world. (All 15 million of them versus 6.5 billion Gentiles!) In countries where there practically are no Jews (Japan, for instance), the Jews are cited for causing market fluctuations, poverty, etc. The Jews have been scape-goats from time immemorial, and we can see the same phenomenon in ancient Egypt when they were slaves, and throughout the A.D. centuries in Europe and the Muslim nations. The Jews were supposedly responsible for the bubonic plague, having allegedly poisoned the wells. They were not getting the plague as readily as the Gentiles simply because they were obeying Old Testament customs about washing the hands before eating, keeping the latrine a certain distance from the kitchen, and other sensible recommendations. Prob-ably the Jews of the Middle Ages were more in tune with biblical reasoning than the more advanced and worldly Jews of today.

Anti-Semitism has cost certain nations a great deal. A list of just Russian and German Jews who fled Europe during 20th century pogroms and Nazism would read like a who's who of science, medicine, and the arts. Names like Horowitz, Rubenstein, Irving Ber-lin in music, and Einstein and others in science, give some idea of the eminence of the Jewish contribution to a host nation. The entertainment industry could be said to be almost dominated by Jewish people in

America. PBS has aired a two-hour program on Jewish comedians, and they could ride in a long parade. It is hard to imagine a two-hour program on Arab humor or that of any other minority group.

It is possible that Europe has been weak in the second half of the 20th century because of the elimination of so many of its Jewish people. Not to be chauvinistic, but the Jews in some cases were the cream of societies in Europe as far as intellectual contributions went. Germany may have been first among those, ironically enough.

Prejudice against the Jews is common everywhere, including contemporary America, where the country club mentality sees them as less worthy associates. Is it Jewish exclusivity or Gentile bias that causes these troubles? Jews have had to build their own country clubs and their own "YMCAs." The author attended a YM&WHA while growing up (that is, Young Men & Women's Hebrew Association, a duplicate of the YMCA built with Jewish funds for Jewish kids).

Jewish food is a phenomenon that is well-known in most cultures. In America, the famous delicatessens are seldom really kosher, but simply serve an Eastern European diet associated with the Jewish ghettos. Delectable "gourmet" items like corn beef and pastrami originally came from salted meats being preserved by people with no access to refrigerators. Jewish ghetto poverty has led to some interesting inventions. But

here again, prejudice of a peculiar kind can happen.
The Orthodox look down on such restaurants. An
Israeli restaurant, owned and operated by immigrant
Messianic Israelis in Dallas, was closed by five rabbis
who took an ad in the *Texas Jewish Post*. They simply
said that they did not recommend the delicatessen,
and virtually all of its Jewish business dropped. Of
course, what they found so unpalatable was the belief
in the Messiah, not the food. It is doubtful those rabbis are perfectly kosher themselves. We ran an article
about this situation entitled "Rabbi, Why Do You
Hate Me?" in our ministry newsletter. One reader, in
response to the article, traveled from Tennessee to have
lunch at this delicatessen, but the place eventually
closed, all the same.

The "kosher" concept is unique to Jews (although
various other groups do observe some dietary restric-
tions), and stems from the dietary laws given by God
through Moses. Here again, though, Jewish law has
departed from the intent of Scripture to the extent
that the modern practice is almost incomprehensible
when compared to its original form. A central ele-
ment of kosher observance is the total separation of
meat and dairy products, which can be traced back to
the command in Exodus 23:19 that forbids cooking
a baby goat in its mother's milk. Dr. Thomas McCall,
our staff theologian, wrote his theological dissertation
on sacrifices in various cultures, and he noted that

pagans sacrificed in this rather cruel manner, and that is why Jews were told not to do this.

But religious leaders have embellished on this command to the point that meat and dairy products cannot be served in the same meal or prepared with the same dishes. The dishes themselves must be segregated, and kept in separate cupboards or in different areas of the house. In some Orthodox homes, there are even two dishwashers — one to wash "meat" dishes and one for "dairy" dishes, so that the two do not ever come near each other. An Orthodox Jewish woman must have four sets of dishes: one set each for dairy and meat, as well as one set each for the Passover meat and dairy dishes (which can only be used during the eight days of Passover). This particular kosher practice has led to two kinds of restaurants for observant Jews — one that abstains from dairy foods and one that abstains from meat. Or if separate buildings are not possible, some restaurants have a line drawn on the floor or a rope strung across, with one side serving meat and the other side serving milk products. Even those Jews who do not follow other kosher laws will often observe this particular prohibition. For instance, my mother never served milk with our bacon.

I am not writing against the observance of the dietary laws given through Moses, which concern clean and unclean animals. God had good reason for commanding His people in this way, as modern nutritionists

have certainly discovered. But this particular observance is an extreme example of what happens when
people do not understand the Scripture. Following all
the myriad laws of the Talmud can give an outward
show of holiness, and can persuade people that they
are righteous before God; but as Scripture itself has it,
it is the heart that is important to God. As Jesus said
to the religious leaders of His day, "Woe unto you,
scribes and Pharisees, hypocrites! for ye make clean the
outside of the cup and of the platter, but within they
are full of extortion and excess" (Matt. 23:25).

Lack of sound Bible knowledge creates some
new kind of Jewish manners and mores. There is an
odd kind of Judaism that looks forward to end-times
prophecy, particularly the temple rebuilding, even
as it omits the rest of Bible study. There are Jewish
people in Israel making costumes for worship in the
temple, jewelry for the women to wear, and trumpets
to be blown to herald the services. These activities
celebrate Scripture, and yet the rest of biblical Judaism is of little importance to this sect. Israel by itself
presents some amazing Jewish stories. In some cases,
the Orthodox living there have recreated their European ghettos, albeit in nicer surroundings, by wearing
the costumes and copying the manners and mores
of those three- and four-hundred-year-old societies.
Little boys wear skullcaps and forelocks. Orthodox
women shave their heads in submission when they

marry (and then buy the finest, most elaborate wigs available, along with expensive, florid hats). At the same time, a family living right across the street may detest these mannerisms and look down on all Judaism as a relic and irrelevant. Still another family might try to affect a "sensible" middle ground, worshiping on holidays but otherwise taking a secular, Zionistic view of Israel. It should not be thought that all of the Orthodox are supportive of Israel. Many of them believe the place should not be occupied by Jews until the Messiah comes, and they are actually anti-Israeli, to the extreme of even drawing swastikas on walls to represent the government as being tyrannical like the Nazis were! Most will not use the Hebrew language, and consequently speak the Yiddish of the ghettos, a remarkable rebirth of an agonizing period in the long story of Judaism.

The question of real faith is complex. I once sat at a Sabbath dinner in Jerusalem where I marveled at the speed with which the family slammed their way through the prayers at the table. I could not help but point out that God himself would have trouble understanding the diction when people were reading like auctioneers, and my hostess began talking about her beliefs. Ultimately she said, "I don't have to believe in anything, I just have to read these prayers." That is an extreme statement of how law overcomes faith, and works are the whole religion.

The manners and mores of a four-thousand-year-
old people are impossible to explain in this space, of
course, and I hardly think I have done them justice.
But it should be appreciated that there is something
called the Jewish way, which operates in the Jewish
community and has always done so, from the ancient
days to the present. That peculiar Jewish style exists
from the Old City of Jerusalem to the Warsaw ghetto
to Brooklyn to the New City of Jerusalem, and is always a separated society, rich in lore, poetry, music, art,
etc., but totally sealed off from both the Jewish and the
Gentile sides. The wall separating Jews and Gentiles
seems to have a plaster surface on either side and the issue of each other's faith is barely understood at all.

And finally, the manners and mores of the Jewish people are simply not based on the Bible. That is
remarkable since, as we have pointed out, the Bible
is wholly a Jewish book. One would hardly expect
sacrifices to be done in an age when there is no valid
temple in Jerusalem to receive them, of course, but the
Bible (or at least the Old Testament) has its own Jewish style, which simply no longer appears. Devoutness
is a concept which is simply not seen in the Jewish
community; rather, there is adherence to Talmudic
law and obedience to European patterns of worship.
Simple belief in God seems to be lacking. Worldli-
ness, condemned throughout Scripture, is considered
almost a virtue in the Jewish community.

Once again, the error is concerned with lack of Bible knowledge.

So if modern Jews no longer live according to Scripture, why should believing Christians support them? Why should they support Israel?

The reasons are numerous, starting with the fact that God chose them as His people. The covenant He made with Abraham was an everlasting covenant, and God will never abandon it. Their current unbelief was predicted in Scripture, as was the grafting in of believers under a new covenant.

As Christians, we should also support them because they are the people of our Lord. Jesus was born a Jew, lived as a Jew, and died as a Jew. When He was resurrected, His salvation became available to all people, but His earthly ministry was directed to the Jews, His people, and His heart now is that they come to know Him.

We should support Israel because God established it as the land for His people, and that is as true today as it was then. Let me give the reasons why Israel is Jewish land. Israel is entirely Jewish land because:

(1) It was given to the Jews by God through Abraham. "For all the land which thou seest, to thee will I give it, and to thy seed forever" (Gen. 13:15).

(2) The history of the place shows the Jews living there for 3,500 years, from long before there were any Muslims in the world.

(3) The archaeology in the land is entirely Jewish. There
    is no archaeology from Arab builders before the 7th
    century A.D. when the Muslims arrived.

(4) The whole world saw Israel win the land in a battle
    imposed upon them by the Arabs in 1967.

Even conceding the first three considerations above to
biased reporters, if land doesn't go to those who won it in a
battle, then we American immigrants had better start packing.

We should also be concerned about Israel because it is
central in end-times prophecy. The Tribulation begins with the
Antichrist's treaty with Israel, he will take over the Temple in
Israel, and the cataclysmic end of the Tribulation will occur in
Israel. Israel is God's timepiece.

But Israel is under attack from many directions. God
stated that they would be hated of all nations, and it is certainly true today. This book will detail the contributing factors to
this situation, from the outright hatred of the Muslim world,
to the duplicitous dealings of our government and media, to
the failure of our education system to turn out true thinkers,
to the failure of the Church itself to understand Scripture and
end-times prophecy. Dark times are coming, but in the end
God will prevail and take His people to a glorious new home
— Israel.

CHAPTER Three

THE MUSLIMS —
THE TAKEOVER
OF AMERICA

Obviously, the Muslims are taking over our country. Anyone who can't see this is burying their head in the sand. When my wife and I spoke recently in Minneapolis, we learned that there are 50 mosques there. (I doubt if there are anything close to 50 synagogues or 50 real Christian churches there). In some communities, public schools are being utilized to change our thinking so that we can become like these people who live in the Dark Ages. The world is heading toward an utter catastrophe if the Lord tarries.

We're not the only ones, of course. I've heard Islam described as "an international psychosis" that aims to control all mankind. And it's not so much the inflexible religion or even

the terrorism that is to be feared, but the day-by-day extreme
subjugation of women, antiquated ways, horrific courts and
punishments, and the return to an unsuccessful society of a
thousand years ago. Americans may yet be seen in our streets
missing hands and feet. Teenagers may die in floggings of
as many as 85 lashes, as happened in Iran recently. Young
women will be hanged, or worse, for bestowing a goodnight
kiss.

After Bill Clinton's unsuccessful foray into Somalia,
the Muslims took the place over and established *shari'a* law.
Subsequently, they assembled 13 thieves in a stadium and,
to the enjoyment of the crowd, leisurely sawed off each hand
and foot in a long ceremony of screaming and what they
pretended to be a triumph of righteousness. This will be common in America if we keep dithering about these people. They
are apparently pouring across the borders from Mexico and
Canada, and I've heard it estimated that there are some 15
million Muslims in America. That would be about five percent
of our total population. In Europe, 5 percent of the population has virtually taken over and changed the political policies
in France, Germany, Holland, and England, to a great degree.
We have many politically correct Americans who imagine that
some Muslims are moderates, but a moderate Muslim was
recently defined as one who had not yet had his chance to
violently overthrow a government.

A liberal-thinking friend in New York City today e-mailed
me the following: "There are over a hundred mosques right
now in the New York area. So what?" I answered that this

would give him quite a choice when the Muslims force him to worship with them.

No one seems to ask why the Muslims are spread out among the blue (Democrat) states in the United States — New York, Minnesota, Michigan, etc. Dearborn, Detroit, Flint, and many other northern cities' populations have a preponderance of Muslims. And that is odd because the Muslims are desert people. After all, they're not familiar with snow shovels or tire chains, and they would be much more comfortable in the South. But, as I have reported, a friend of mine from Oklahoma stated, "If they tried to pull that stuff down here, we'd run 'em outta town." The fact is, liberal Americans throw out a red carpet for everyone with the best of intentions, but do not comprehend the difference between this minority, which wishes to take over our nation, and the others that are benign.

It's no joke. Not only are there imams preaching "death to America" and calling us "the great Satan" on our own soil, but we even have their professors in some of our key universities. They teach much the same philosophies.

Recently, this ministry resisted the incursion of one of these Islamic "intellectuals." I wrote an article for our February 2005 newsletter:

The Trouble With Tarry

I was so shocked and disappointed by an article that I found in the December 6 *US World and News*

Report that I sent them this editorial. In the story by
Jay Tolson, which covered some four pages, the magazine all but weeps over the fact that potential Notre
Dame professor Tariq Ramadan will not be joining
that faculty at all due to the U.S. State Department
"Acting on advice from the Department of Homeland
Security" revoking his visa. The opening page bears a
picture of a rather handsome, athletic-looking Muslim
with a deeply concerned expression. The article specifies that despite various pretenses, he is as radical and
dangerous an Islamic operative as one could find, even
on an American university campus.

One of his credits refers to him as a "gentle
jihadist," and the article states, "If not an advocate
of violence, his detractors say, Ramadan provides the
ideological seedbed of a highly politicized Islam — Is-
lamism as it is called — in which more violent forms
can take root." Citing that Ramadan, typical of many
Islamic speakers, talks differently depending on who's
in the audience, the article states, "Islam condones
dissimulation in dealing with 'unbelievers.' " Dissimulation means, according to the Internet dictionary,
"To disguise (one's intentions, for example) under a
feigned appearance," but in this case it's garden-variety
lying.

The would-be professor is the grandson of the
Egyptian activist who founded the bloody Muslim
Brotherhood. "There is a miasma around him," says

Daniel Pipes, director of the Middle East Forum in Philadelphia. "You can explain one, two, three, four, five things. But finally, when there's so many charges, you can't explain everything away. We don't need him in this country."

That's the issue — discussion over whether this particular Islamic professor is radical enough to do some damage or whether he's worth hearing from. But now comes the part I was complaining about. Writers Anna Mulrine in Berlin and Elizabeth Bryant in Paris join Tolson in stating, "The controversy clearly weighs most heavily upon the man and his family, but it has much wider implications. Above all, it raises questions about how America, and the West in general, are engaging in the struggle for the hearts and minds of the Muslim world."

That's the part that confuses me. I didn't understand that we were in a struggle for the hearts and minds of the Muslim world. I thought we were trying to keep the Muslim world from continuing to murder us. The writers go on to say, "It is hardly news that a decisive conflict is underway in that global community (of Islam) with a small but well-financed minority hoping to make its absolutist and puritanical construction of religious law (or *shari'a*) the foundation of an all-encompassing political and social order." Well, personally, I wouldn't say that shari'a is any particular "construction of religious law." Shari'a is the stuff where they behead folks, hang young girls for acting romantic, cut out tongues, etc., etc. This is no "absolutist and puritanical construction" of anything. It's barbarism. It belongs in a jungle of ten thousand years ago.

The article goes on to say, "The question, of course, is how America and the West can identify and encourage those other Muslims — particularly intellectual and clerical elites — who see the radical Islamist agenda as a betrayal of the true spirit of traditional Islam and an unworkable blueprint for future states. . . ."

Well, yes, there I do agree. I really do think World Trade Center attacks, mass graves, totalitarian dictatorships, enslaved millions and hundreds of millions, and the like really are "an unworkable blueprint for future states." I would prefer that our own states, the United States of America, once they're taken over by Muslims, not follow that blueprint. (The takeover, as I've said many times, is well under way.)

A professor at The Institute of Political Studies in Paris talks about "the deplorably politicized state of Middle Eastern and Islamic studies in the United States, where much scholarship divides into simplistic pro-Arab or pro-Israel camps." Well, I've never heard of a pro-Israel camp at any American university, where I always volunteer to speak in the hopes of promoting fairness to Israel. What are known as Middle Eastern and Islamic studies in this country are simply Israel-bashing forums. This is too obvious to even articulate.

The issue surrounding Professor Ramadan was settled for me toward the end of the article when the then French Interior Minister Nicholas Sarkozy debated Ramadan in November 2003. The minister "challenged him to call for the abolition of the stoning of women for adultery, a practice considered Islamic according to some fundamentalist interpretations of *shari'a*. Ramadan . . . refused to issue a blanket condemnation, calling instead for a moratorium on the practice so that its legitimacy could be debated among learned Muslim scholars and jurists — the *ulema* — throughout the world."

Well, that settled it for me. I don't know about you.

What a difference from Jesus, who was presented with a woman taken in adultery and simply said, "I do not condemn thee." I guess the "learned Muslim scholars and jurists" are without sin and can cast stones.

The most irritating part of the article was the highly partisan writing, deeply championing this odious Islamic scholar with statements like, "The pity of excluding Ramadan on the grounds that his ideas might be dangerous, many believe, is that it seems to reject the American confidence in the marketplace of ideas." That's just politically correct gibberish. If anyone believes that the stoning of human beings has any credence in "the marketplace of ideas," he needs to see a psychiatrist. Yet, Ebrahim Moosa, a professor of Islamic Studies at Duke University, objects to the whole discussion on the grounds that it is "a velvet glove inquisition that insists on what can or cannot be a proper conversation on Islam in the modern world."

If I hadn't thrown up my hands before, imagine my reaction to "If there is something inherently incompatible between the fundamentals of this spiritual formation (that is Islam as, above all, a spiritual discipline) and the ideals and institutions of free, liberal societies, then Ramadan does not see it."

In the last paragraph, the *USN&WR* editorializes with reckless abandon: "The cost of shutting out Muslim thinkers such as Ramadan could be very high for America if the nation is really committed to winning the long-term war of ideas behind the war on terror." Once again, I'm mystified. I didn't realize that we are in a long-term "war of ideas" with the Muslims. Once again, I thought we were trying to prevent them from continuing to kill innocents, including school children, and from taking over country after country in order to subjugate the whole world into their cockamamie system. I just wonder what ideas are on their side of this "war of ideas." If we have an idea that people should be free, what is the competing idea from their side, and what can we learn from it?

The New York University law professor Noah Feldman, author of *After Jihad: America and the Struggle for Islamic Democracy* and a former constitutional advisor to the Coalition Provisional Authority in Iraq, supplied the following propaganda: "We can only learn what we need to know about contemporary Islam if we have a chance to encounter people like him (Ramadan) in our universities. Unless a person is an active security threat, excluding him or her from an academic visit is shooting ourselves in the foot." No. A thousand times no. Encountering people like him in our universities is what is causing the awful subversion of our values and our youth.

And if excluding that sort of professor from a major university is shooting ourselves in the foot, well I think that accepting him is simply shooting ourselves in the heart.

Let's go back for a moment to the attack on Pearl Harbor. It was not as destructive as the one on the World Trade Center, sinking ships and murdering some 2,400 innocent souls. Moreover, it was an attack on a military base, not on civilians. But it was the same sort of sneak attack by a sworn enemy. Did we then allow the Japanese to establish their temples in America? Did we reach out to them as part of our democracy and our care for minorities, etc., etc.? No, rather we placed Japanese in this country into internment camps. That is considered a very black moment in American history. But although many innocent people were affected, there were no casualties, and we probably inadvertently took off the streets a thousand potentially dangerous terrorists.

The problem in America is that we are accommodating an enemy so vicious as to put the Japanese, the Germans, and all previous enemies in the shade. Had we been taken over by either Germany or Japan, we would at least have remained in the 20th century and we would have been very uncomfortable being occupied by foreign forces. If we are taken over by the Muslims, we'll be lucky to survive at all and only lose some limbs and some innocent civilians.

One concept that seems to escape present-day analysts is that the Muslims have been undermining and taking over other nations for 13 centuries. Since the beginning (Mohammed was born around A.D. 570), they have conquered 22 Middle Eastern nations, including the powerful, then highly Christian nation of Egypt, and Indonesia in the Far East, with its 238 million souls (now mostly Muslims). They have made inroads over time into almost all of the eastern hemisphere, and now they are taking on the western hemisphere in all seriousness.

Egypt is comparable to the United States, because in its time it was the world-dominating culture. The Egyptians, of course, built the pyramids long ago, did brain operations, sent fleets on the high seas, perfected astronomy and mathematics still useful today, and virtually dictated life and death to the known world of their time. After the coming of the Lord, the Coptic sect, Egyptian Christians, became very strong in Egypt.

But over all this time, desert people were riding in, as poor people will, into a culture that was better off. When those desert people became Muslims, something new happened. They determined to take over all of Egypt and they accomplished it, so that in the 20th century it was finally renamed The United Arab Republic.

And so the once world-dominating culture could not even feed itself any more.

Patrick Cox, contributing editor to our ministry newsletter the *Levitt Letter* and editorialist with *USA Today* and many other publications, contributed recently the following thoughts on the story of the Muslim takeover of Egypt, published in our December 2004 *Levitt Letter*.

Resisting Egyptian Dhimmitude

This September, a truly historic meeting took place in Zurich, Switzerland, aptly named the "First International Symposium on Egyptian Copts: A Minority under Siege." To understand how momentous were this gathering and its plea for the international community to help protect Egyptian Christians, some background information is necessary.

The image of Egypt that most of us share today is that of a relatively poor Islamic desert country, barely able to feed itself. There was a time, however, prior to its conquest in the year 641, when the Christian nation was the breadbasket to Rome and Constantinople. The

port city of Alexandria was, at once, home to the greatest scientific library of antiquity and the capital of the
Christian world.

Native Egyptians, descendants of the same people
who built the pyramids, embraced the teachings of the
apostle Mark in the first century and prospered as the
civilized and wealthy people known as "Copts." Their
affluence and artistry were an irresistible lure to Arab
and Persian marauders, and Coptic control of the
region was ended by the same wave of conquest that
put Syria and Palestine, using the Roman word for the
Jewish homeland, under Islamic rule.

For a period, Egypt's new Arab rulers reaped a
bonanza of tax revenues from the prosperous Copts,
but it was only a matter of time before the top-down
control of society, for the benefit of the ruling elite,
reduced the region to the borderline poverty that still
afflicts Egypt and most of the Muslim world outside a
tiny oil-rich minority.

The Copts were reduced to second-class status in
their own ancestral lands, at times providing enough
value to the Islamic rulers to buy their safety, but
always suffering when the attitudes and policies turned
against them. Throughout the centuries, the Copts
of Egypt have been, in the words of Daniel Pipes,
"among the more meek of dhimmis," using the Arabic
word for an officially inferior class of people living
within an Islamic nation.

Coptic acceptance of this subservient status should not, however, be attributed to a lack of courage. Copts represent only 10 percent of the Egyptian population and, traditionally, those who have complained about their treatment have suffered serious retribution, including imprisonment and assassination. When criticism has come from outside the country, Egyptian authorities have at times retaliated against Copts within their borders.

The symposium in Zurich, therefore, demonstrates dramatically the international Coptic community's realization that the plight of the six million Copts in Egypt is worsening and that something must be done, despite the risks, to protect them. Tellingly, there are fewer Copts now than there were when Egypt was conquered in the seventh century. Several million have fled the officially sanctioned discrimination and periodic pogroms, and an estimated 700,000 live in America alone.

Many historians, in fact, trace the roots of modern Islamist terrorism to Egypt in the 1920s, just as the other major totalitarian philosophies of the 20th century, communism and fascism, were evolving in Europe. It is interesting, historically, to note that Egyptian Islamists had a cooperative relationship with Germany's Nazis.

The virulently anti-Christian and anti-Jewish Muslim Brotherhood was founded there in 1928, and

by the 1930s all the hallmarks of modern Islamist
persecution had taken shape. Egyptian schools began
teaching that Christians and Jews are inferiors whose
only worth is serving Muslim needs. Non-Muslims
were systematically excluded from important government and university posts. Bans or long delays in
permission for church construction, or even repairs,
were enforced.

Squads of Islamist thugs, who engaged in attacks
on Christians and their businesses, were constituted,
often with the knowledge and protection of local
police. Subsequently, hundreds of Christians died at
their hands.

Alarmingly, the frequency and seriousness of
assaults on Copts and their property has been increasing. According to human rights activists, including
Pope Shenouda the Third, the kidnapping and forced
conversion of attractive Christian girls has become
commonplace, dozens disappearing annually never
to be seen by their Christian families again. Whole
Christian villages have been burned and looted,
though law enforcement authorities have routinely
failed even to seriously investigate incidents of anti-
Christian violence.

Those who follow affairs in the Middle East will
have, by now, recognized the pattern. This degrada-
tion and mistreatment of non-Muslims is widespread
and common in Islamist territories, best evidenced

by the continuing outflow of Christians from the region.

Of the millions of Christians living in Turkey at the beginning of the 20th century, only a few thousand remain. Most Syrian Christians have fled their homeland, as have their Lebanese brethren. Poignantly, so many have fled persecution in lands controlled by the Palestinian Authority that Bethlehem and Nazareth, once predominantly Christian towns, are now almost entirely Muslim, and unsafe even for Christian tourists.

The only country in the Middle East, in fact, that is experiencing a steady growth in its Christian population is Israel proper, having seen an increase from 34,000 in 1949 to more than 120,000 today.

There are important lessons to be learned from the ongoing persecution of Christians at the hands of Islamic theocracies. One is that we cannot count on the Western media to provide as much coverage of the massacre of hundreds of thousands of modern Christians in Sudan, Pakistan, and Timor as it does the accidental deaths of Palestinian civilians when Israel retaliates against terrorists in Gaza and the West Bank.

I wonder, in fact, if this blackout on news of Islamic persecution of Christians does not stem, at least in part, from fear that it will disprove the lie that Israel has provoked, somehow, the hatred of its Arab neighbors. In fact, we must come to grips with the fact that a fierce, at time genocidal, racism is endemic in much of the Islamic world. The assault on the Jews of Israel must, therefore, be seen as simply one part of a much larger and older effort to force all non-Muslims into the humiliating capitulation of dhimmitude.

The problem, of course, is spiritual. Bible students fully understand that God has an enemy and that enemy takes many forms. In the case of Islam, it is taking the familiar form of replacement theology; its goal is to replace both Judaism and Christianity, and frankly, it's well on its way. The battle, however, is the Lord's, and in the end, both Israel and the Church will prevail. Still in all, there's a long time of difficulty to go before God's triumph at the end.

While not all Muslims are violent, we can't overlook the murderers and complicit murderers that make up an unfortunately large portion of the society. You can't excuse the ones that aren't terrorists just because they don't participate themselves. They give money. They are sympathetic. And on the whole, they support them. What is it in Muslim spirituality that turns these people into murderers and usurpers of other people's territories? As to that, we've seen it all before. The Nazis had an ideology and attempted to take over the world. Hitler declared that his Third Reich would rule for a thousand years. Stalin and the communists likewise had some arcane theory of how things might be run economically, sharing and sharing alike, etc., but in the end, it was the same old song and dance. They took over other people's countries and stole their

wealth. Had they not finally broken their teeth on Afghanistan, we might still be trying to cope with a world gone largely
communist. The Japanese were part of the same story earlier in
the 20th century, with their attempted takeover of many Asian
countries.

It is not some kind of dearth of spirituality that makes
Muslims do what they do, so much as the simple human lust
for power, wealth, and the next fellow's land. With that said,
however, it certainly never helped anyone to worship a false
god or purvey strange, inhumane ideas as a religion. The world
is packed with religions. Even Christianity is subdivided into
a polyglot mixture of sects. But at least all of them pronounce
the name of the Lord, and they, at least recently, are not hostile
to anyone. Muslims have been hostile to everyone since their
inception, and that suggests something truly satanic in the
works. Their very faith forecloses all other faiths, so that they
must conquer the Jews and the Christians to please their god.
This is inimical to other religions. The world just doesn't operate that way under normal circumstances.

Rev. Ed Hindson has advanced an interesting theory that
since the church does not know when the end will come, neither, in fact, does the devil. And so Satan must prepare a whole
cast of characters for an upcoming Tribulation, technically,
in every seven-year period. And so we had the Japanese, and
then we had the Nazis, and then the communists, etc., and,
most recently, Saddam Hussein, Yasser Arafat, and the Muslims. They have been ready just in case. Should the Antichrist
hear his cue and step forward, his henchmen will already be in

their places. Or, in the analogy of a play during its last act, the stage is already set, the characters are saying their lines, and the Antichrist and his thugs are waiting in the wings, listening for their cue.

Obviously, all of that spiritual data is unknown to the U.S. government, the U.N., etc., and in fact, unknown to most Christians, other than those who truly study Scripture (a mere remnant). Truly, it appears that Islam does not have to "sneak up" on the nations. It can do this robbery in broad daylight with few to forecast it or appreciate what's really happening.

Frankly, if the Lord tarries, it's all over for us. Until He comes, we will increasingly become a Muslim-dominated society like Egypt is, and we will deteriorate in the same manner.

The Muslims tend to sneak up on you. In Europe, they have been moving in for decades, and now represent about 5 percent of the total population of the member states of the European Union. That doesn't seem like much, but in view of the fact that almost every one of them is noisy and indignant and full of outrage, they make quite a tumult in any society. If Turkey is accepted into the European Union, that will quadruple the percentage of Muslims to 20 percent, some 100 million souls.

We have shown how the United States is being infiltrated with imams in mosques built by Saudi Arabia, preaching "death to America" and calling us "the great Satan." This goes on under the auspices of the Wahhabists, the most radical of the Muslims, and it is an undisguised national takeover like that which we detailed earlier of Egypt.

Certain commentators, very knowledgeable about Islamic tactics, have described what's really going on. Steve Emerson, an expert on terrorism, has quoted from Islamic sermons and kept a close eye on these people in America. Itamar Marcus, an American expatriate to Israel, keeps an eye on the Palestinians from his offices in Jerusalem. They both agree on one thing: these people are up to no good.

We can use all the "denial" we want, and we can talk about political correctness and making our American Muslim friends feel at home, etc. They are still infiltrating our nation and intend to take it over. They are not just another American minority. They are the enemy, and they have already attacked us. It should not be necessary to say this, but in the strange climate of liberalism that pervades our thinking on this subject, people have to almost be reminded that we are at war. Our "war on terrorism" is not exactly that. It's a war on Islamic fundamentalism. There are no other active terrorists but Muslims.

They are subtle and they win your confidence, as with Mahmoud Abbas. This henchman of Arafat's, now supposedly a peace-loving "Palestinian" "president," has in mind the destruction of Israel just as his mentor did for the 40 years in which he tormented the Chosen People. But Abu Mazen (as he's also known) unfailingly appears in a suit and tie, unlike Arafat, and he is relatively soft spoken and seemingly agreeable. Of course, he was chosen to be ineffective; Arafat would not have selected a really strong second-in-command for fear of his job and his life. But now that Abbas has that job, Israelis are very watchful, and with good reason.

Lately, the Muslim infiltration has become obvious in America, and in a way, they're no longer sneaking up as much as thumping their chests with righteous indignation and demanding power in the American democracy.

They are welcome to such a place, but only if they act like other American minorities. Participate, vote, build the country, and support it.

But if you plan to undermine it and take it over, you are the enemy, and you should be treated as such.

It's no secret that the Arabs are a concern to the entire world. To get the figures right, they comprise something near one-third of all Muslims. Their territory stretches from the Atlantic Ocean to the border with Iran. (Iranians are actually descended from Persians, albeit fundamentalist Muslims to rival any.) There are 350 million Arabs, at some reckonings — Arabs don't take accurate censuses. Nearly every one of them is taught to hate Israel and talks about it all the time.

This whole idea is sort of ridiculous. It's like all the people in the other 49 states being taught to hate New Jersey, which is about the size of Israel, when New Jersey has done nothing to earn the hatred. I don't have to make the point again in this section that Israel has done the Arabs no wrong, and of course it bears repeating that it would do the Arabs no end of good if they would simply accept the Israelis as neighbors. After all, the two sides lived together for thousands of years.

It is the fundamentalist brand of Islam, Wahhabism, that is mostly responsible. "Normal" anti-Semitism pervades every nation, but this is a special, intensive hatred that is taught to every child as if it were some religious doctrine. (It varies in the Koran, which sometimes praises the Jews as "people of the Book" and sometimes despises them as infidels.) Christians are not spared this hatred either, but the Jews possess a very tiny country in the midst of what Arabs like to call their nation, and are regarded as a kind of tumor on the place.

In reality, Israel, of course, out-produces all 22 Arab nations combined (except for the oil that was discovered and developed by the British and Americans), has won an enormous number of Nobel Prizes for its size, and does the Arabs no bad service whatever. The world can rail all it likes about the trumped-up Palestinian situation, but that is a very small issue and one propagandized out of all proportion.

With all of that said, it should be observed that when Arabs come to Christ they are exactly the same as other believers — Jewish, WASPS, Europeans, etc. Born-again behavior is exactly that around the world. They believe in the same Lord, read the same Scriptures, and behave in the same ways. Their lives are improved by the Lord in exactly the same patterns, so that when one approaches a group of foreign Christians, one is immediately impressed with the peace and good fellowship. We indeed become one *mishpocha*, as the Israelis would say, a family.

I'll never forget the day that I was teaching my tour group in the Upper Room in Jerusalem. I tried to keep my remarks brief since other groups kept coming in as we stood there looking at the Scriptures. There were people from Nigeria,

Korea, South America, Sweden, etc. I concluded the lesson and I took out my recorder and we broke into a chorus of "Amazing Grace." At that, all of the groups began to sing that great hymn, each in their own language!

What a Pentecostal scene! Everyone singing the same hymn, looking around and smiling at each other — folks of nations whose leaders may be involved in all sorts of animosity, yet with fellow Christians, there was perfect harmony. That was a small picture of the Kingdom to come and it was most heartening.

My point is that there could just as well have been a bunch of Iraqis, Egyptians, Syrians, etc., all of whose nations contain Christians. (There wouldn't have been Saudi Arabians because Christianity is so suppressed in that backward and primitive country that they would have been afraid to demonstrate their faith in public. The punishment is ordinarily death, and sometimes death by torture, for believing in Jesus Christ in Saudi Arabia.)

On my program, I have interviewed any number of Arab and even Palestinian believers, including Anis Shorosh, Louis Hamada, Ergun Caner, Zak Hanani, and, more recently, Walid Shoebat. Every one of them was a kind Christian believer with a very good Bible knowledge and, of course, a fascinating testimony. Hanani and Shoebat were formerly terrorists, and Shoebat actually delivered a bomb one day against an Israeli bank in Bethlehem. (No one was hurt, since when he saw children in front of the bank he threw the bomb up on the roof instead of walking in with it. Even as a young terrorist, he had a heart, which is not typical of young Palestinian terrorists.)

Shorosh, Hamada, and Caner are all theologians with a great deal to say about the Bible from a perspective we do not usually hear. In fact, Shoebat spoke on my television program on the idea that the Tribulation protagonists would mainly be Muslims. He developed this notion with a wealth of scriptural references referring to old Arabic names of territories with which he was very familiar. It was a perspective we don't usually get.

Shoebat is a converted Muslim who is accepted in the synagogues as a speaker, and churches are becoming more familiar with his important message. The synagogues in this case are ahead of the churches in their concern for Israel and its future. They see the Holy Land already attacked by Muslims, and they are spellbound by this affecting speaker's point of view. As to the churches, they are behind on the study of prophecy, as we emphasize elsewhere, and they do not appreciate that the current world situation, vis-à-vis Islam, is leading right into the end times.

In summary, when a human being begins to believe in Jesus Christ, he is indeed, as the Bible says, a new creature, and as a corollary to that thought, he becomes a creature just like all the other creatures who believe in the Lord. Obviously, the Lord changes lives and inspires people because they come out all the same! And that goes for Jews, Gentiles, and even Arab terrorists. In the end, the answer for the Muslims is the answer for all of us — salvation through Christ.

THE PALESTINIANS — A MYTHICAL PEOPLE

Although we discuss the Palestinians elsewhere in this book, the subject needs a comment in its own right. Most people seem to be unaware that there are no "Palestinians" as described by our media. Palestine was a made-up name imposed on Israel by the Roman Emperor Hadrian in A.D. 135 in yet another futile attempt to wipe God's people from the earth. And until the nation of Israel was re-established in 1948, *all* residents of that land were known as Palestinians, certainly the Jews. There was no distinct Arab group known as Palestinians.

Until it became convenient, that is. That particular myth surfaced in the 1960s and has been a very useful propaganda tool for those who want to drive Israel into the sea. Although archaeology has clearly proven that Israel was originally established more than three millennia ago, the "Palestinians" claim that it is their ancestral land and that it is being illegally occupied by the Israelis. The world has bought that lie, even to the point that outright terrorists are considered "freedom fighters" struggling valiantly against an oppressive regime. Even the most heinous acts — shooting a pregnant mother in front of her four daughters, blowing up schoolchildren, targeting teenagers out for a pizza with their friends — are smoothed over or outright ignored.

The latest dodge to cover over Palestinian atrocities is to try to lump in that future terror state (if the Lord tarries) with those of brighter prospects like Iraq and Lebanon.

The March 14, 2005, *Newsweek* magazine was devoted to its cover headline, "Across the Arab World . . . People Power." An article by Fareed Zakaria entitled "Where Bush Was Right" follows the encouraging developments in certain of the Middle Eastern dictatorships.

But one must be careful exactly what one swallows with this whole glass of water. Writer Zakaria says this: "Most ordinary Arabs, it turns out, are not consumed by grand theories about the clash between Islam and the West or the imperialism of American culture or even the Palestinian cause. When you let the Lebanese speak, they want to talk about Syria's occupation of their country. When Iraqis got a chance to congregate, they voted for a government, not an insurgency. When a majority of Palestinians were heard from, they endorsed not holy terror to throw Israel into the sea, but practical diplomacy to get a state."

The last three statements are a classic example of mixing a lie in with some truth to make it fly. The statements about Lebanon and Iraq are certainly true. The one about the "Palestinians" is utterly fabricated by this Arab writer. Palestinians did not have a free election at all. As I have pointed out repeatedly, their dictator died and they were made to go to the polls and appoint his number two man as their new dictator. The fact is, Hamas, the terrorist group with blood all over each hand, was the big winner in that "election."

Poll after poll taken in "Palestine" shows that not only do the vast majority of people want to "throw Israel into the sea," but they also want to continue killing innocent Israeli civilians *after* a two-state solution!

It should also be noted that these people refused a state when it was presented to Arafat on a silver platter.

When you read these sentences make sure they're all true, particularly when a fellow named "Fareed" writes in the American media. The subtlety and duplicity of many Arab and Muslim reporters is designed to, and many times is successful in, slipping past gullible readers lies, disinformation, and propaganda.

In the same manner, Muslim professors at our great universities indoctrinate our brightest youth with many of the same tricks. Of course, on a university campus, they no longer have to be subtle at all. We're not far from learned symposiums on subjects like "Exterminate Israel," "Kill the American Jews," etc.

Obviously, a two-state solution, with Israel side-by-side with terrorists, would be no solution at all. So why would our leaders put forth that hopeless Roadmap to Peace? I addressed that question in our April 2005 *Levitt Letter* in "Enough Rope":

> I have been wracking my brains as to why reasonably informed people like Condoleezza Rice and George Bush would favor the creation of a Palestinian state. Obviously, there are no people in the world less qualified than the Palestinians, who basically have no economy, no trade, and almost no skills to operate a new nation.
>
> Palestinians are very dangerous people. The majority of them have committed themselves to murdering their Israeli neighbors whenever they can. The Israelis have restrained them by building the protective fence, but presenting them with new borders, plenty of space, possibly air and sea depots, and the like, obviously is not a reasonable plan for peace.
>
> But then an idea occurred to me. Sharon and Bush are both notably clever tacticians, and the Israeli prime minister, an experienced general, certainly understands the inherent dangers in our Roadmap. What if the two of them have tacitly agreed that they will cause this new state to happen in order to give the Palestinians "enough rope." They may mean to provoke a premature attack instituted by a new sovereign state from within its own borders.

It's like a sacrifice in checkers. You allow your opponent to jump one of your men so that you can jump two of his.

When attacked, the Israelis, then arrayed along the Mediterranean coast, would have no recourse but to defend themselves with all they have. They will certainly not, as Golda Meir put it, "commit suicide so that the world will speak well of us."

They will wipe out the attacking Palestinians, and that should take care of the problem once and for all.

And how then could the world complain? At this point, they accuse the Israelis of an occupation, bad treatment of a minority, etc., but when the Palestinians have their own country, they certainly can't accuse the Israelis of those things.

And perhaps that's the "real" peace process.

In the chapter on Muslims, I mentioned former Palestinian terrorist Walid Shoebat, who is now a believer. On our TV program with Shoebat, taped before Arafat's death, I tapped into his experience growing up and being educated in the West Bank. I described to him my own limited experiences in "Palestinian" cities.

My wife and I visited Ramallah where I interviewed Hanan Ashrawi, and she treated me courteously. But what we could see around us, well, there's no reason for this kind of suffering. There's no reason at all. With Arab money and Jewish brains, the Middle East would be paradise.

Exactly. But instead, in Ramallah, what they did was make a massacre of these two reservists. Remember the story of the two reservists? Now, here's an argument. These two reservists who got lost, it's not an Arab culture tradition to kill them. You show them the way. Instead, here the entire city of Ramallah participated in the lynching of these two guys, gouging the eyes, taking the intestines, putting them on a board and then praising Allah in the streets. It's one thing if a cult does something like this. We understand this, it happens here in the states. It happens everywhere. There are cults and groups that do all kind of crazy things. But when an entire city participates in such a cult act, this speaks volumes. This says that this Nazism with a religious twist, called Islamic fanaticism, has really permeated the Middle East. The Middle East is plagued with this mentality where 80 percent of Palestinians support suicide bombing and all the children want to become suicide bombers. This is a disease now that is out of control. It has to be stopped. We can't create a Palestinian state if this status quo continues. How could you have such a state where the people are acting like cannibals?

Now, Walid, let me take you there. All right, the Roadmap says there's to be a Palestinian state by 2005. Now, if you made a state out there, how would it operate?

Yasser Arafat's job, that is clear. We will have an Arab state with Islam as the state religion. That means Jews can't live there. Converts to Judaism or Christianity can't live there. It's really an Arab state. And they say Israel is a racist country! Well, in Israel proper, there are Jews, Muslims, and Christians, blacks, whites, and Orientals. None of the Arabs want to give up their Israeli passport. Have you heard of any Arab that wants to give up their Israeli passport and go to the Yasser Arafat's territory? In fact, in my entire family, Zola, we had a family reunion in San Francisco. I asked them, how's life now under Arafat's rule. They said, "It's awful." Then I asked them, how was life under occupation. "Those were the good old days." Then why don't you speak out? They said, "You're asking a silly question. We will never live under Jewish control. This is something that's in our blood. We will always refuse Jews to be rulers."

Even though it works.

Even though it works. And now, Zola, I always say, I pray for the occupation so we can have peace.

Obviously, the "occupation" that any believer prays for is that of the coming King in the thousand-year Kingdom centered in Israel.

Dr. Ergun Caner, recently appointed dean of Liberty University, Rev. Jerry Falwell's college, has appeared several times on our television program. He is especially knowledgeable of

Islam, being the son of a muezzin (the guy up in the top of the minaret that calls everybody to prayer) and the author of a book called *Unveiling Islam*. He was a very religious Muslim holy man, and he came to Christ. He really knows his stuff.

There are Muslim professors, like Tariq Ramadan, and there are Christian professors who used to be Muslims, like Dr. Ergun Caner. Below is some of what Dr. Caner shared with me on the program.

Why would we want Jerusalem?

Well, I'll tell you by telling of one of our holidays we celebrate. I am not a Muslim, now, of course, but I say we, because these are my kinsmen. And so, like Paul's heart, in Romans 9:1–3, I wish that my kinsmen would be saved. The Muslims would celebrate Ediata, which is commemorated by a three-day feast every year, Abraham taking his son to the top of Mount Moriah, getting ready to sacrifice him, the knife comes down and surprisingly Allah provides a ram in the thicket. When I got saved by Jesus, I was amazed to discover that the Genesis 22 story is Abraham and Isaac. Because we in Islam believed it was Abraham and Ishmael. It was one small change, one small editorial change. If you think about it, huge parts of the Tanach, the Old Testament, are in the Koran. But they pick and choose. Mohammed picked what he wanted to go in there. Genesis 12, the covenant is not in there. It's not Abraham, Isaac and Jacob, and Joseph, community will be permeated by some of the "salt of the earth." One can only hope.

As the Chinese philosopher said with an explosive double meaning, "May you live in interesting times." We certainly do.

of course. It was Abraham and Ishmael. But in the story of Genesis 16, Sarah, not God, tells Abraham, "I want you to go in to my handmaiden because obviously I am barren. I want you to be intimate with my handmaiden." And so, Abraham, like a very good husband, says "Well, if that will make you happy." Then Ishmael is born. So, because Ishmael is 14 years older than Isaac, they think they have the birthright of the oldest son. And they think that the site where they have now built the golden dome mosque is the Abraham and Ishmael, the sacrifice of Ishmael. And so it is 2,700 years after it took place, 2,200 years after Moses wrote it under the inspiration of the Holy Spirit. They changed the story. And so, I felt somewhat betrayed, when I became a believer in Christ, to read so much that had been taken out of the Bible and made to fit into Islam.

Dr. Caner and I further discussed how Islamic people practice their religion, and I came to the following conclusion. This is just a religion of works.

Absolutely, complete and total works. Every thought, deed, motivation, desire, everything goes onto one scale or the other scale. Only one thing erases the bad scales eternally: martyrdom and jihad. So, the people who died at the World Trade Center bombing felt that by shedding their blood and other people's blood (2,800 other people's blood), they would purchase their eternal security.

It's terrifying when you think about it.

They weren't particularly holy men. By all reports they were fooling around days before they did this terrible mission, eating, drinking, and being merry, because tomorrow we will be forgiven. Indulging in liquor and women, right before doing the holiest kind of mission, to hear the press talk about it. And you read in the letter they found in Mohammed Attah's luggage that didn't make it onto the plane. The Protocols they followed in the moments before they hijacked the planes were explicit from the Hadith, specifically volumes 4 and 5. They did Weblu, the ablution, blowing on themselves, reading the Koran. Everything they followed comes from the Hadith. All the times I've spoken since September 11 — you and I are extremely busy people, you much more than me — but still one time I was speaking, the Muslims were yelling, and one man was yelling "You are betraying us," because no one has ever put Islam under the microscope like we and others have been doing.

I may say there are very few believers in Christ, totally knowledgeable of Islam, like you are.

I'm much obliged sir, but I wish there were more people interested when 1 out of 5 people that walk this earth are of the Muslim mentality. It's one thing to say, as American Muslims do, "We don't believe in jihad," so

they may seem to be a peaceful people. But it's q[...] other to say that jihad is not found in the Koran, [...] jihad is not found in the Hadith, because right n[...] speak, there are 300,000 holy warriors, jihadin, u[...] being trained. I'm talking about being trained ana[...] to die in a holy war. It's something that's incumben[...] us to know. This will balance their scales, in a sense, [...] is the road to salvation.

It's their only hope, is it not?

Well it sounds that way. Nobody died for their sin[...] They're not paid for. I think everyone at the end of the[...] day, Dr. Levitt, looks back at their day and sees more[...] bad than good. I mean, if I was depending on my own[...] righteousness, I would think of all the thoughts I'd had, [...] all the things I'd done, all the things I'd said harshly. An[...] I think the Muslims have this midnight cry of their soul[...] where we think, "Ah, I've done more bad than good. It's[...] hopeless." And then you tell them, "Ah, but what if by[...] one act in one day you get total forgiveness and, by the[...] way, 70 virgins are waiting for you." It's a promise. It's so[...] opposite. First they sin, then they do this terrible act and[...] they're absolved. And they get up to paradise and they sin[...] some more.

In any case, Caner, Shoebat, the other converted Muslims I mentioned, and hosts of others who are "in the closet" give one a bit of hope that the large Islamic

THE GOVERNMENT —
RENDER UNTO
CAESAR

Render to Caesar things that are Caesar's, and to God the things that are God's," said our Lord (Mark 12:17), and indeed, we are to be much more concerned with the next world than this one.

I get letters to the ministry asking why I don't comment more on American politics and why I don't appear to care what goes on in Washington. Actually, that's not exactly the case, I tell them. I care, of course, as a born and bred American. But I'm fully aware that should the Rapture come today (or before you finish reading this paragraph), America, in effect, will be "no more" for me and all the other believers. We will instead be escorted to heaven and then to a thousand-year Kingdom in

Israel. We'll then proceed to spend eternity in the "new" Jerusalem on a "new" earth under a "new" heaven (Rev. 21).

And that, in effect, is why I am more focused on the Holy Land than on America. But with that said, I was delighted with the results of the last election and I take President Bush to be a believer. I think it makes quite a difference. Journalist Cal Thomas recently pointed out that he felt that Bush and Condoleezza Rice were of the same faith (he didn't say which one, but I think it was the same as Cal's own faith).

I believe Bush got his bad reputation with unbelievers everywhere when he simply called evil "evil." When he pronounced that Iraq, Iran, and North Korea comprised an "Axis of Evil" powers in the world (and could anyone now doubt that?), he was telling the simple truth. Our Lord pointed out that the truth would set us free and that those of the truth would follow the Lord.

It's just as true that those who are not "of the truth" do not follow the Lord and, in effect, hate those who do. It's back to the Cain and Abel people again. The world is divided into these two kinds of people, and the Cain people invariably kill the Abel people, or at least they hate them with all they have. And so, a perfectly reasonable president doing a perfectly creditable job, protecting this country and doing what he can about terrorism elsewhere, is maligned, hated, insulted, and considered a moron practically around the globe. Notwithstanding, he continues to make the world a better place.

I voted for Bush, but this is not to say that I'm carrying posters. I am skeptical of most any government, and I'm appalled by his first-term statement, "I have a vision for a Palestinian state." One does not have a vision for something like that. One may have a nightmare about that, but not some hopeful dream. It's not that I oppose the Palestinians as Palestinians (they're not really "Palestinians" at all, but simply illegal Arab aliens, the majority of whom crossed the borders when the Jews were building a new nation from 1948 to the present) — it's that dividing an already small land experiencing so much strife is obviously a recipe for war.

The best solution is to wholeheartedly support Israel's right to its land, undivided and uncompromised by Arabs' demands.

The gospel teaches that one cannot serve two masters, and that is obvious as life goes on. The United States government is trying to please both the Saudi Arabians and the Israelis.

In the first case, we are dependent on the Saudis for oil, and we seem to kowtow to that awful regime. It is remarkable that a democracy like ours would take seriously the Saudi "royal family," thousands of multimillionaires who have pretty much stolen all of their country's oil wealth, leaving the rest of the population to fend for themselves. The close relationship between the Bush family and the Saudi princes cannot help but give one pause, and the idea of the president having a Saudi prince as a houseguest on his ranch was simply atrocious. Shortly before that, 15 Saudi hijackers joined 4 other lunatic terrorists in attacking the World Trade Center and the Pentagon. I suppose on that occasion the president was trying to demonstrate that we do not hold all nationals responsible for the terrorism of a few, but his gesture was overdone. It did not take into consideration the constant Saudi exports of Wahhabism and the rest of the dangerous fundamentalist Islamic gibberish.

At the same time, Israel is undoubtedly our best ally in the whole world, and a thriving democracy. We cannot help but support it for what it is, to say nothing of the fact that America has a long and mutually beneficial relationship with the Jewish people. What is known as the "Jewish lobby" consists of personalities who are trustworthy and well-accepted in Washington circles. There is no question that the United States and the Jewish people have gotten along well for some two centuries while Arabs have been strangers to us. The Arabs were not necessarily enemies until the World Trade Center, but they had no record of heritage in the United States, either. Statements of American loyalty by Arab agencies like CAIR (the Council on American-Islamic Relations) exaggerate their relationship with America. It is entirely based on oil, and should some other energy source be found, I believe there will be no relationship left.

Through the various U.S. administrations since modern Israel was founded in 1948, different presidents have taken different points of view toward that ally. In general, Presidents Nixon and Reagan seemed understanding of Israel's problems. Clinton and the first George Bush were less sympathetic to Israel. George W. Bush, president at this writing, seems mostly positive toward Israel and certainly never had anything at all to do with Arafat, whom Clinton consistently invited to the

White House. Clinton seemed totally fooled by Arafat and the Palestinians, or perhaps he just didn't care one way or another. But George W. Bush accurately labeled Arafat a terrorist and entirely refused to meet with him.

Through all of this, the State Department was less understanding of Israel or, as they might put it, "more evenhanded." The idea is that the diplomatic corps, who must get along with all governments, thought they could play it down the middle and be friendly with Arab nations and also a friend of Israel. And there would be no reason why not if the Arabs would themselves accept Israel as a good neighbor. But such State Department officials as James A. Baker, author it is said of the Roadmap to Peace, were downright hostile toward Israel, and certain diplomats, after their terms were up, became actual paid spokesmen for the Arabs. Edward Abington, in plain sight, took pay from the Palestinians to represent them, and Edward Walker, after his stint in Saudi Arabia, fronted that nation in Washington. These two prostitutes, if I may use the accurate term, evidently would say anything for anyone for money, and that's what they did.

And the talk is all about a controlling Jewish lobby in Washington!

In general, the State Department has not been friendly to Israel, and under Colin Powell, and now under Condoleezza Rice, is repeating the same patterns as in the past; there are fake peace conferences, fake handshakes, fake photographs, and fake congratulations. And all that fakery is followed by very real rockets and car bombs.

The American people, supposedly represented by their government, have in general a favorable outlook toward Israel, but are persuaded by the media that it is a dangerous and war-torn place. Very little could be further from the truth but, convinced of that, they become suspicious of Jewish people in general and, of course, of Arabs who have actually attacked them. The government nevertheless goes along willy-nilly, conducting diplomatic relations with Arab dictators and despots of all sorts and mouthing benign platitudes about the misbehavior of Iran or Syria or Saudi Arabia or Libya as they go.

In a nutshell, because of their oil, the Arabs enjoy a disproportionate acceptance in Washington at the same time as they arouse a great deal of suspicion and real fear among the American citizenry.

That fear is justified. Many in our government seem oblivious to the increasing Muslim influence in America. As I wrote in our January 2005 *Levitt Letter*, "A Note from Zola":

We might do well to watch what's happening in Europe, and particularly Holland, with the ongoing Muslim takeover. Reasonable people everywhere have written off France, Germany, and England on bad days, as utterly lost to the Muslims, and not real allies of ours. In Holland, the enemy has taken a further step, murdering a filmmaker for questioning their treatment of women, and then terrorizing by means of arson, beatings, and killings in their host country. As in the United States, these Muslim immigrants were originally welcomed. Holland has sown the wind and reaped the whirlwind. Their political correctness has come back to haunt them.

We're doing much the same. Obviously, such violence will begin to happen in the United States if we don't do something about the Muslim incursion. This is a much larger country and the Muslims are progressing more slowly here, but the takeover is running according to schedule. As an example, we could take the recent pronouncements of James Zogby, brother of pollster John Zogby, an Arab American. He remonstrated with us for criticizing Arafat and calling him anything but Abraham Lincoln and George Washington wrapped into one. He is among the first to cry out when Muslims feel what they call discrimination, but is silent when they murder children in Russia or Israel, or murder anyone anywhere else.

The larger problem here is that Muslims not only are encouraged by their religion to lie, they are guilty of believing their own lies. When I interviewed such personalities as Faisal Husseini or Hanan Ashrawi, I listened to seemingly normal human beings lying through their teeth in the most obvious manner, and yet sounding very sincere in all that they said. They were forthright and used persuasive language and what they considered reasonable arguments to pronounce the most unbelievable and far-fetched falsehoods. But they seemed to believe their own lies. Hanan Ashrawi's statement, "Jesus Christ was a Palestinian prophet born in Bethlehem in my country," is really hard to beat. She claims to be a Christian woman.

This situation reminds me of the story of a Muslim fellow who was trying to take a nap while some children were playing outside his bedroom window. He finally yelled out of the window, "You kids go to Muhammed's house. He's giving away free candy." The children ran away and the man resumed his nap. But in ten minutes he was in the living room. His wife said, "I thought you were going to take a nap," and he replied, "No. I'm going over to Muhammed's to get some free candy."

The sickening part of what's going on globally is that the United Nations, and even elements in our own government, are friendly with the Muslims whose plan is to take us over. Political correctness is one thing, but embracing an enemy who has already attacked you, is plain stupidity. Such organizations as the U.S. State Department, with its endless tolerance for dictatorship, terrorism, and the like, and the Presbyterian Church USA, are examples of liberal foolishness.

In an earlier chapter I gave the reasons why Israel is Jewish land. Here I'll proceed to explain a scenario of the Tribulation that might occur if the proposed Roadmap is actually implemented.

The Roadmap proposes establishing a Palestinian state in the midst of Israel in the year 2005. At this writing, we have just entered that year, and are therefore about to undertake this catastrophic idea.

As I explained above, my assumption, going by all past history, is that as soon as the Palestinian state is established, it will attack Israel more ferociously than it does now. And, with the Israelis arrayed along the Mediterranean coast, the attacks will be deadly serious. Israel, for its part, will not back up obediently into the sea to please the United Nations, the president of France, or whomever. As a matter of fact, I think they will get out their weapons, of which they have many, and will really settle with the Palestinians. It will be a total defeat for the attackers, and Israel, of course, will survive just fine.

However, this disaster will provide an excuse for the other Arabs to avenge the losses and they will come en masse to invade Israel. This will perhaps be the invasion called Gog and Magog in Ezekiel 38 and 39. The powers named in that invasion are all Muslim. In verses 38:5–6, Ezekiel specifies Persia, Ethiopia, Libya, Gomer, and Togarmah. "Persia" represented a huge conglomerate of nations in Ezekiel's time, including parts of Afghanistan and Pakistan on the east, and Iran, Iraq, Syria, Jordan, etc., a huge force that could attack Israel from its north. "Ethiopia" may represent the whole southern contingent of Sudan, Somalia, Ethiopia proper, etc. Libya is well-chosen as an antagonist of Israel and will gladly play its part (despite present declarations of peace and the supposed taking down of weaponry). The last two allies, "Gomer" and "Togarmah," are thought to respectively express the areas of eastern Europe around the Danube Valley and the Caucasus north of Turkey, both Islamic areas these days.

And our own incursions into these areas would be a prime motive for the attackers, in addition to Israel's defeat of the Palestinians. It's interesting that each and every aggressor comes from an area that we "provoked" in some way. Persia was provoked when we went into Afghanistan and Iraq. With regard to Ethiopia, we invaded Somalia. With regard to Libya, we bombed Gaddafi's very roof some 20 years ago. With regard to Gomer, we certainly found plenty of Muslims in the areas of Yugoslavia, and we were criticized for defending them but, in any case, we did. And we offended Togarmah when we asked Turkey to allow us to place an army that would have invaded Iraq from the north at the beginning of the Iraqi war. They declined (even when we offered something like $30 billion) since they realized that someday we Americans might pack up and leave and they would still be sitting there with some half a billion Muslim maniacs near their borders. So, in a sense, we will inadvertently help bring about the Gog and Magog invasion with our Roadmap.

When that invasion occurs, God says, "My fury shall come up in my face" (Ezek. 38:18), and, in the end of Ezekiel 38:

> For in my jealousy and in the fire of my wrath
> have I spoken, Surely in that day there shall be a great
> shaking in the land of Israel; So that the fishes of the
> sea, and the fowls of the heaven, and the beasts of

the field, and all creeping things that creep upon the earth, and all the men that are upon the face of the earth, shall shake at my presence, and the mountains shall be thrown down, and the steep places shall fall, and every wall shall fall to the ground. And I will call for a sword against him throughout all my mountains, saith the Lord God: every man's sword shall be against his brother. And I will plead against him with pestilence and with blood; and I will rain upon him, and upon his bands, and upon the many people that are with him, an overflowing rain, and great hailstones, fire, and brimstone. Thus will I magnify myself, and sanctify myself; and I will be known in the eyes of many nations, and they shall know that I am the Lord (Ezek. 38:19–23).

Notwithstanding, the world doesn't give up on eliminating Israel, but rather forms up the invasion of Armageddon in which virtually all the world comes down on little Israel.

They still don't get the job done. The Lord, who said, "And except those days should be shortened, there should no flesh be saved" (Matt. 24:22), comes down from heaven, puts a stop to Armageddon, and starts the Kingdom on earth.

In Israel.

And thus, the American government has a lot to do with the upcoming Tribulation, if only inadvertently. In reality, we're trying to do good things, spreading democracy and freedom, overcoming radical Islam and its strictures on so many societies. But God's plan marches on and prophecy will be realized.

America has always prospered as long as we accommodated the Jewish people and supported Israel. While there is some anti-Semitism around, and all Jews have felt it, America has been far kinder to the Jews than any other nation where they have lived, as I said previously. I could go on and on about the brilliant Jewish brains cast out by Russia, the eastern European nations, England, France, Italy, etc., and of course, above all, Germany. How many Einsteins, how many Jonas Salks, how many Rodgers and Hammersteins, Jack Bennys, Isaac Sterns, and on and on, were killed in that hideous Holocaust by the Germans? How many wonderful lives were lost, not only to the Jews, but to all mankind? As my own brother put it once, "Europe remains weak because they killed out their cream." (And now, to add insult to injury, the "missing" Jews have been "replaced" with millions of Arab immigrants.)

Our government could have done much better during the Holocaust. We turned away ships of fleeing Jews, and we were not always kind to those who made it here. On the other hand, we didn't murder them wholesale, and we allowed them a chance to excel. And excel they did.

I won't go into detail about what magnificent contributions Jewish people have made to the American culture, but suffice it to say that our government did much better than other governments in allowing these people to be free and to accomplish what they could.

And after all, the Scripture declares them "a blessing unto all nations," and they will be just that when permitted to do so.

The government acts scripturally in still another way. Our income tax and many other taxes effectively transfer money from the rich to the poor almost in the manner of the ancient Israelite civilization. In the year of Jubilee (Lev. 25:10, etc.), slaves were set free, mortgages were cancelled, and everyone reverted back to zero, so to speak. The biblical Jewish culture admitted to no "old money." There were not aristocracies of oil men or real estate magnates or political dynasties due to a certain inherent fairness promoted throughout the Old Testament. Usury laws were strict, and the poor were compensated in whatever ways possible.

Another way the government is helping God's plan along is its war on terrorism. It obviously helps Israel for our diplomats and our armies to go after these antagonists of freedom and democracy. As dangerous as our flirting with a Roadmap to Peace may be in Israel, we are still impressing our enemies on all sides with the very real threat of taking down their regimes or influencing them to at least be more democratic. Any moves toward democracy in any Muslim states will accrue to Israel's benefit, just as Wahhabism and the other Islamic excesses operate to Israel's detriment.

No small influence in America is accomplished by the born-again believers, called "the religious right" by the media. I like to think of those who helped move this election toward reelecting the president as simply people of common sense, many of whom happen to be biblically motivated. But in any case, ours is no small voice these days. And that, I think, is a phenomenon of the end times.

The prophets picture a polarized kind of world as the end draws near. Believers have their faith, and unbelievers have their unbelief. In other words, people are choosing sides very emphatically in today's world. Our government seems to be mostly in the hands either of Christian people or at least those who respect the Judeo-Christian values that are obviously a major part of American history. And that is a great comfort. Just as the president can accurately call evil "evil," he can just as accurately call good "good." Since the end times are given as a period when unbelieving men will call good "evil" and evil "good," the believers will call them what they really are. Israel is good and the U.S. government seems to know it, and despite the opinions of the rest of the world, the United Nations included, American people, at least evangelicals and those who voted with them, know that Israel is good.

Israel is a sister democracy, a valued ally, and a most progressive nation. It's one of only a handful in the world that have put up a satellite, or that have nuclear weapons (for good reason). Its unquestioned contributions to the world in the way of curing diseases, providing technology, and being a constant example (in the middle of an ocean of Arab dictatorships) that democracy is far and away the best method of government — even in the Middle East — are heartening.

God chose these people to be "a blessing unto all nations," and they are. And as long as our government supports Israel and promotes its freedom, stability, and security, we will prosper.

Before leaving the subject of the American government and its policies, I must reiterate a position that has been advocated in the *Levitt Letter* for some 25 years. I feel it is absolutely necessary that we change the regimes of Saudi Arabia, Iran, and Syria, at a minimum, in the Middle East. The longer we dither, the worse things get.

Saudi Arabia is exporting Wahhabism as fast as it can, building mosques around the world, and promoting terrorism. We must stop that. When your basement is flooded, step one is to shut off the incoming water. As to Iran, of course, it is building nuclear weapons and that is an intolerable situation. No matter what it takes, we have to stop that process. And Syria is a hotbed of terrorists' headquarters, an endless supplier of insurgents on the ground such as those in Iraq, and a hiding place for Saddam's weapons of mass destruction, I assume. The Syrians mean nothing but harm to those around them and to the free world. Their chief business is drugs, and if they could conceivably arm enough to damage Israel, they would go ahead and attack her immediately.

When I say "change those regimes," I do not necessarily mean in the Iraqi model. We may well not have to march into Riyadh, Tehran, or Damascus. For instance, we have witnessed recently the withdrawal of Syrian troops from Lebanon, apparently in response to Iraqi elections. And sometimes diplomacy will work, but it has to be of the sort that allows no other alternative. It's time for the dictators to ride out of town and their governments to fall. They could be reconstituted any way these countries desire, but at least that will take time and cause some disorganization. In that time, we may be able to make inroads against world terrorism, which will have its financial and personnel supply lines seriously compromised.

In plain words, if we told the Saudi royal family "the game is over," and that if absolutely necessary we'll move in, I think they would listen to reason. And when the common folks saw the Rolls Royces leaving the capital, they would not be radicals anymore.

If we go ahead and take down at least those regimes, to say nothing of Egypt, Libya, Sudan, the southern Russian republics, and so forth, we would have a real war on terrorism which would make some real headway. Failing that, I'm convinced we're going to lose, if the Lord tarries, and the whole world will go into a new Dark Age, the like of which has not been seen in world history.

CHAPTER Six

THE MEDIA —
PURVEYORS
OF TRUTH?

A major source of misinformation about Israel is, of course, the media. While news organizations at first seemed supportive, or at least factual, about the fledgling nation that was born of such tremendous effort and courage, over the decades their reports have degenerated into sensationalist depictions of Israeli "atrocities" and calls for it to capitulate to the terrorists that threaten it. One could well wonder how these self-styled "guardians of the truth" could have reached this state of affairs, but recent scandals have offered a glimpse into the inner workings of the media machine. How the information powerhouses have handled these transgressions is very telling.

Recently, Fox News ran a story about the *New York Times* as it recovered from the Jayson Blair scandal. Blair of course was a very young — right out of college — black reporter who was evidently hired by the *Times* in response to affirmative action. The *New York Times* invariably follows a liberal line and practices liberal policies, and hired a completely inexperienced reporter.

Blair was atrocious. He fabricated stories, made up interviews, and often tarnished the front page with utterly false information. That was nothing new to the *New York Times*, as faithful readers know; the *Times* has an awful reputation for distortion despite being "our newspaper of record."

When Blair was caught, it caused an avalanche of reader response saying, "Serves you right," and "That's what you get for your constant distortions. You finally went a step too far." I personally cancelled my subscription to the *New York Times* more than 10 years ago after 20 years of faithful reading. I simply could no longer stand the slanted coverage of Israel, and I thought to myself that if the information is so badly biased on a subject I know, then what sort of coverage am I getting on subjects I don't know?

The *Times* responded by holding august conferences on the question of "How can we get more credibility with our readers?" Meetings were held and important journalists were consulted, and a great many fine lunches were eaten, but the *Times* never stumbled over the fact that they could simply tell the truth. To date, they have not changed any of those policies of bias of which they are daily accused. In the end, they stated that they would use fewer "anonymous sources" (how could anyone believe a newspaper that says "an anonymous source disclosed . . ."?) and try to hire better people, etc. They refused to admit to a liberal bias, rather like Dan Rather or CNN, and instead took their lumps, like Dan Rather and CNN.

Our point here is that the entire investigation was false. It was simply done to impress subscribers that the paper takes their complaints seriously, when it really never does. Lately, there's a new look to investigations of wrongdoing everywhere. They are biased, false, and misleading, and they come up with foregone conclusions by partisan investigators.

At press time, *Newsweek* took over for those other unworthies with its utterly false report of a Koran being flushed down a toilet by American interrogators. Apart from the ensuing deaths and horrific rioting by Muslims in several places, *Newsweek* never really expressed regret at the incident. They reluctantly retracted the story with the same old double-talk. It's really hard to say just which of the very unpatriotic American media that we have cited is the worst, but *Newsweek* is surely in the running. It conducted the usual false investigation, of course, and excused itself summarily.

The U.N. "Oil for Food" scandal (allowing Saddam Hussein to gain money that he funneled to his war machine) is a prime example. The "investigations" are going on right now, even though it has come out that Paul Volcker, who heads those investigations, has business connections to those he's investigating. He spent months gathering data. In the end, despite billions of dollars missing, he seemed to find no real fault with Secretary General Kofi Anan, who was evidently elbow deep in the mechanics of this particular scandal. We'll probably never get to the bottom of this because the false investigation will do its work, it will indict nobody important, and it will reach the conclusion that everyone had good intentions and no one did much of anything wrong.

The investigation of the sleazy Dan Rather story, using false documents to slander President Bush's National Guard service, was another case in point, of course. In the end, Rather continued to broadcast — a pathetic wounded bird flying alone to jeers and well-earned derision. One article I read on that subject asked why no one went to jail for trying to subvert an American election. And that is a good question. It's hard to imagine a more history-changing crime. But, in the end, the investigators found "no political bias."

What a horselaugh! The entire situation was political bias from start to finish, and the whole world knows it. But the investigators, again cronies of those at CBS, simply asked for the resignations of three individuals and the firing of a fourth. To this date, the three have not resigned and I guess we're all trying to put this in the past and get by with the punishment of only one underling. The situation is pathetic and has a devastating effect on all network news. No one would argue that Peter Jennings is unbiased, but he simply hasn't been caught. Tom Brokaw has retired before committing any transgression along these lines. And otherwise, CNN, MSNBC, etc. — all but Fox News — can be painted with the same brush as CBS. Obviously, they are biased to the liberal side. They are against the president and his policies, and they frequently host guests who are biased as well.

If they're caught in something, they will immediately start up an "investigation." This will stall for time and also come up with a non-indicting conclusion.

I think the public is just not that stupid. I think that it makes people angry to see behavior like that on the part of organizations we used to trust.

A related journalistic crime is that of plagiarism. Several celebrated journalists, including Doris Kearns Goodwin, were accused of simply copying passages from other publications and taking credit for writing them. When caught, they give a silly laugh and say, "Why, I had no idea. Yes, I read that other writer, but I didn't realize his ideas influenced me to such a degree." That's absurd. When one copies word-for-word from a different copyrighted source, it's a crime and there aren't any excuses other than saying, "I was too lazy to do my own work and I collected royalties for copying someone else's." It's hard to see where that particular larceny differs from stealing some other individual's invention or piece of music or any other creative endeavor, and falsely taking pay for it. We don't even bother with investigations when plagiarism is the topic. We simply listen to a half-baked excuse and move right along.

A larger and even more troubling system of false investigations involves our courts. Anyone who has ever been in litigation is nonplused at the way lawyers talk in depositions and in trial. They are evidently there to obstruct the law, to obfuscate the facts, to posture as if they don't understand the plain words of an individual talking to them, and to distort reality until, by hook or by crook, they can get their client off and take an enormous fee for that. Personally, I collect "lawyer lies," the sort where, for example, police indicted for shooting down an unarmed suspect are defended by a lawyer saying they thought the victim was firing at them and their bullets accidentally ricocheted. All 42 of their bullets.

A more recent example of a lawyer fabrication that was downright amusing was the individual defending one of the soldiers involved with the Abu Ghraib prisoner abuse. When dealing with the issue that his client forced naked prisoners to form a pyramid, the attorney exclaimed, "Why, cheerleaders make pyramids all the time!" Such utterly unethical prevarications discourage us all where the law is concerned.

One would think that people who have come out of a graduate school such as law school would be above telling the sort of lies that get these knee-slapping guffaws, but they are not, and we are becoming inured to that. Our courts are simply a running joke among business people who go to any lengths to avoid every sort of litigation.

It's false investigations that are being indicted here. Never mind all the unethical behavior and all the lying and all the fixing behind the scenes — and all the bribing, also common to our courts. The whole idea is that someone competent is going to adjudicate a dispute according to statutory law, and finally, the Constitution, and we're supposed to believe that when we see the performances we actually get.

I watched a long CSPAN interview with a brilliant young writer named Thane Rosenbaum. He has written a book called *The Myth of Moral Justice* and makes much the same point as I am making here. There just is no moral justice left, and the sad fact is the United States probably has the best system of justice in the whole world. The chicanery, these overpaid attorneys who joke behind the scenes with each other on different sides of a case and "fix" the facts, and these judges who pretend not to understand the testimony but simply convict whom they please, and sentence them as they please, constitute the best human legal system ever devised! What a falsity of investigative procedure and what injustice!

We could compose a hundred books this size of false government investigations. This particular dodge has been a mainstay of Congress since the beginning of the United States. If somebody important is caught at something, a grand investigation is held, and months or years later he is found half-guilty perhaps, but the citizens have long ago moved on to new issues.

Our subject, however, is the media, and the fact that, as with the courts, we start to get a deep feeling of distrust, and finally a feeling of being betrayed, and those feelings are justified.

On the subject of Israel, that brave young democracy running like a watch, and utterly successful from the day it was re-founded in 1948, has been totally excoriated by the world media. I can only think of the *Wall Street Journal* and the *Washington Times*, offhand, which tell something close to the truth about that nation. I have, in other chapters, gone to some lengths to show that the reporting of danger to visitors, etc., is false. And, finally, the very idea that this nation is a threat to peace — a current fashionable complaint about the Chosen People — is beyond absurdity.

If the whole world operated as Israel does and the media simply left it alone and did not cover it, there would be utter peace there. Israel would undoubtedly reign for a thousand years of undisturbed peacetime.

And that's the plan!

A current example of the media's irresponsibility and its overwhelming impact is the reportage from the war in Iraq. While it is clear that this operation has been a major success, considering the democratic election and only sporadic resistance to our troops, much of the media, taking the line of the Democratic party apparently, are savaging the entire operation.

The *New York Times* is especially guilty, and, of course, other newspapers dutifully copy its articles, and TV news people clip its thoughts for broadcast. The error is not so much one of misreporting facts — a car bomb is a car bomb and casualty figures are casualty figures. But there is a distortion of scale. Bad news is purposefully exaggerated. As with the reportage from Israel, the majority of the media emphasizes what negatives there are and invariably leaves the public with a very disheartening picture.

One reason the news has the tone it does is that the major players such as the *Times*, AP, Reuters, and so forth, utilize the services of "stringers." These "misreporters" are usually a necessary evil, but evil they are. I wrote the following piece recently for our ministry newsletter.

Stringers Who String Us Along

On the occasion of the recent car bomb in Lebanon, the front page of the *Orlando Sentinel*, and probably any number of other newspapers, had a dramatic photograph by Muhammed Muheisen and a story by Mohamad Bazzi, both of the Associated Press. It occurred to me, as a former newspaperman, that we should lay some stress on the idea of using "stringers" — local "newsmen and photographers" — to get our facts.

You see, the Associated Press, an American news agency, pretends that its reporters are everywhere at once and that they cover all news personally, but the fact is they rely on local suppliers, especially in countries where freedom of the press is limited.

And, obviously, these local news people come with local biases. The story of the car bomb is objective enough, but what really happens in Iraq or in Israel is open to some interpretation. Those areas contain American news people since Israel proper and occupied Iraq have freedom of the press. But areas within those countries where the press is shackled, say Fallujah or areas outside of Baghdad and certainly "Palestine," have to be covered by locals.

All news from Palestine is originally submitted by Palestinians, along with their views, which usually include a carefully schooled hatred of Israel.

In Egypt, a supposedly moderate Muslim nation, the press is rigidly controlled by the dictator. All that we have said here applies to television networks as well, so that the news we watch from any Muslim nation carries with it the personal prejudices of whoever happens to be broadcasting.

And it gets worse. There are a lot of areas in the Muslim world from which there is practically no news at all. There is little press, free or otherwise, in Sudan, Indonesia, Saudi Arabia, Iran, and on and on. I mention places that happen to be in our news because of world-shaking events going on where information slips out via U.N. workers, foreign medical helpers, or occasional government dissidents. But as for day-to-day coverage in Muslim nations, you might as well cross out over a billion human beings — 20 percent of the world from accurate news reports. Add to those the same number of souls controlled by communism, including all of China, and we have nearly half the world under at least "managed news." Some borderline democracies also suffer from control of their news, as do certain mature democracies like our own.

If I mention a list of Muslim nations, most Americans have hardly heard any news of them. What's going on today in Tunisia, Bangladesh, the United Arab Emirates, etc.?

We complain about American reporters being biased, and some of them surely are biased. Reports from the *New York Times*, CNN, the major networks, and probably your hometown newspaper are almost laughable. The *Times* always requires special mention, since its fabrications are copied by other newspapers far and wide, and even read on television by folks with handsome faces who we are supposed to believe are real news reporters. That's bad. But it's a whole lot worse when newspapers are closed or utterly suppressed, as in Muslim and communist dictatorships throughout the world.

We reported last month that the king of Nepal had deposed his entire government and shut down the press in his nation (where he owns all the land and all the people). Most tyrants are smarter than that. But know that in this world there are despots who arrogate to themselves this kind of power over their fellow human beings.

We may as well count among them some clergymen, including some Catholic priests, some rabbis, and the General Assembly of the Presbyterian USA Church. While they don't close down media outlets, they are all, in their own minds, little kings of Nepal riding roughshod over whatever flock they can control.

As to born-again believers, we have a certain amount of this problem from pompous seminary professors and famous Bible teachers, but it is generally understood that the true Church has no hierarchy. After all, there are only two levels of Christians: One who was perfect went on to His father some 2,000 years ago, and the rest of us are works in progress.

As reported in the February 14th edition of the *National Review*, the staff of the *Jerusalem Post* has performed a valuable task of singling out international news organizations that retain Palestinian Authority employees masquerading as journalists. Among them are the Associated Press, one of whose reporters does work for the PA-financed *Al-Ayyam* and Agence France-Presse, whose Gaza correspondent is also the chief area reporter for the PA's Voice of Palestine radio. Armstrong Williams and the Department of Education have nothing on the world's big media and the Palestinians. With reporting coming from the terrorists themselves, is it any wonder positive news of Israel, or of America even, is hard to come by?

I dealt with one example of media distortion in our October 2004 *Personal Letter*.

As we went to press, the horrific attack on the Russian school by the Muslim terrorists in Russia was in the news. We were disturbed by a certain problem in the reporting of this story. Virtually no news sources specified that the "Chechens" are Muslims. This is another example of politely "excusing" Muslim terrorists.

Ask your friends and associates if they know the religion of "Chechen rebels." Most won't be able to tell you that these child killers are Muslims. The American "mainstream" press do their best to cover the story of the Russian school massacre by Islamic terrorists without mentioning that they are Islamic at all.

> ABCNEWS.com calls them "secessionist Chechen rebels."
> CBS News calls them "militants" and "hostage takers."
> CNN.com calls them a "group" of "attackers."
> MSNBC calls them "hostage-takers" and "Chechen rebels."
> USATODAY.com calls them "armed militants."
> REUTERS.com calls them an "armed gang," and says "It remained unclear who the "attackers" were."

I personally checked the *Dallas Morning News,* and, sure enough, on Friday, September 3, in a half-page article, they went through the entire school hostage story and never once used the terms "Muslim" or "Islam." Any number of euphemisms were used to describe the Muslim terrorists. The next day, the *Morning News* was struck by the fact that it was discovered that some "Arab fighters" were among the assailants. Only then did they relent and use the word "Islamist" for the first time. With their backs to the wall, CBS finally admitted the presence of the Arabs as brothers in arms of the "Muslim Chechen terrorists." But, even Fox News referred to them as Chechens, not as Muslims.

I simply don't understand why we are unwilling to name our enemy, or why we think we must kowtow to the Islamic community with the pretense that they are not violent. All terrorism of any note in the world today is Islamic. All airport security worldwide is there to protect against Islamic terrorism and no other kind. If we don't start to truly know our enemy, I have a fear that we are going to lose impetus in our "War on Terrorism." The term "terrorism," used by itself becomes a euphemism: our War on Terrorism should be called a "War on Islamic Terrorism."

Words like insurgent, fighter, militant, or guerrilla need some definition and should not be used to cover up an identity. (The term "guerrilla" is too much of a compliment for people who attack school children. Guerrillas typically attack military targets. "Fighters" is also giving too much credit. Whom did they "fight?")

Below, I have tried to supply a glossary of terms that you will find in the news regarding terrorism and what each term really means:

1. Insurgents = Muslim murderers
2. Militants = Muslim murderers
3. Guerrillas = Muslim murderers
4. Secessionist Chechen rebels = Muslim murderers
5. Revolutionaries = Muslim murderers
6. Arab fighters = Muslim murderers
7. Rebels = Muslim murderers

8. Armed gang = Muslim murderers

9. Resistance fighters = Muslim murderers

10. Iraqi resistance = Muslim murderers

11. Palestinian freedom fighters = Muslim murderers

12. Assailants = Muslim murderers

13. World Trade Center bombers = Muslim murderers

14. Bombers = Muslim murderers

15. Suicide bombers = Muslim murderers

16. Shoe Bombers = Muslim murderers

17. Perpetrators = Muslim murderers

18. Attackers = Muslim murderers

19. Radicals = Muslim murderers

20. Kidnappers = Muslim murderers

21. Hostage-takers = Muslim murderers

22. Gunmen = Muslim murderers

23. Captors = Muslim murderers

24. Commandos = Muslim murderers

25. Hamas = Muslim murderers

26. Hezbollah = Muslim murderers

And, believe it or not (from the *Pakistan Times*) . . .

27. Activists = Muslim murderers

We consistently catch Islamic "charities" supplying terrorists with cash for weapons and operational expenses. The definition of Islamic "charities" should be: "Those who support Muslim murderers."

The same goes for Islamic dictatorships around the world. Whether they are known enemies, such as Iran, or supposed "partners in peace" such as Saudi Arabia, they amount to another group of "those who support Muslim murderers."

It is as important to use the terms "Muslim" and "Islamic" as it was when President Bush used the term "evil" to describe some of our enemies. They *are* evil, and by that we mean satanic. This is a religious war and one likely to rage in the upcoming Tribulation.

After the Pearl Harbor attack in 1941, we went after the Japanese. The press did not call them "Pacific rim patriots" or "overseas insurgents," or "Far East freedom fighters." We named our enemy, the Japanese, and we fought and won a war against them (and after a difficult occupation, we managed to turn them into a democracy; we accomplished the same with our other enemy, Germany).

For the press, part of the problem today is that George W. Bush named Iraq and Iran (Muslims) in his "Axis of Evil" speech after 9/11. The very fact that Bush included the North Koreans in this speech was a politically correct move to insulate him from the racist (against Muslims) charge. North Korea, with its nuclear capabilities, is surely dangerous, as are many other countries, but I cannot recall a single instance of North Korean terrorism against a western country.

If the mainstream press were to begin using the terms "Islamic" or "Muslim," they would, in a sense, be admitting that George W. Bush was right in his

"Axis" speech. Such confirmation would put Bush in a good light, and that simply cannot be allowed to happen in a presidential election year. Ninety percent of the reporters in the mainstream press are liberals and voted against Bush in the November election. Although they deny their bias, it is plainly evident in their political coverage.

Biased reporting and the accompanying "politically correct" attitudes can make politicians afraid to fight this war. It is not racist to identify the enemy! Ironically, those in the media would be among the first people beheaded in the event of an Islamic takeover of this country. We must recognize our enemy, call it by its real name, and wage an all-out war to defeat it. The West needs to understand that the acts of terror being committed worldwide amount to the mass murder of innocents. Similar to the "Holocaust," the victims cannot protect themselves and they are being assailed by a neurotic ideology. The following article describes the views of an Islamic cleric in Britain:

London Telegraph
"Cleric Supports Targeting Children"
By Rajeev Syal, September 5, 2004

An extremist Islamic cleric based in Britain said yesterday that he would support hostage-taking at British schools if carried out by terrorists with a just cause.

Omar Bakri Mohammed, the spiritual leader of the extremist sect al-Muhajiroun, said that holding women and children hostage would be a reasonable course of action for a Muslim who has suffered under British rule.

In an interview with the *Sunday Telegraph*, Mohammed said, "If an Iraqi Muslim carried out an attack like that in Britain, it would be justified because Britain has carried out acts of terrorism in Iraq. As long as the Iraqi did not deliberately kill women and children, and they were killed in the crossfire, that would be okay."

Mohammed gave a recent interview to promote a "celebratory" conference in London to commemorate the third anniversary of the September 11, 2001, attacks.

The time has come for the civilized world to take a stand against these Muslim barbarians. If necessary, we must use our weaponry and military power to convince the "Saudi Royal family" that further promotion of Islamic Wahhabism will result in their own destruction, not the destruction of the West. They must halt the morbid teachings of violence and death, the slanderous lies about Christians and Jews, and become part of the civilized world. They must stop treating their women like domestic animals, and stop their suicidal "jihad" against the rest of the world.

The results of such distortions are nothing less than the erosion of international support for our efforts to spread democracy, and the pardoning of the terrorists. Obviously, these murderers — akin to Los Angeles gangs — very much enjoy the reward of publicity for their efforts and imagine themselves to be "saving their nation" when they kill our troops. Saying that the entire country of Iraq, or Israel, for that matter, is up in arms, and people are being bombed and shot down everywhere, is a lunatic exaggeration. But it bolsters the efforts of the nether forces.

It also erodes the support our troops get from the people on the home front. With TV newsmen telling of car bombs in their grave tones and *Nightline* piously reading out names of troop casualties, Americans become discouraged. But when compared with the statistics of murders in our own streets or even with traffic accidents, the casualties overseas are minimal, almost miraculously few considering the size of the project and all that's been accomplished. Some 1,500 soldiers have died in Iraq and something over 1,000 Israelis have been victims of Palestinian terrorism. These numbers have to be compared to over 16,000 murders a year in the United States where (apparently) there is no war. Even correcting for population differences, the United States, as is usual when comparing these numbers, is ten times more dangerous than walking down the street in either Iraq or Israel.

For the figures to be really accurate, taking a walk down any street in Israel during the four-year intifada would be some 80 times safer than walking down any street in the United

States in the past four years (about 80,000 killed in four years in the United States versus about 1,000 in Israel). In Iraq, soldiers are more than 10 times safer than they would be in the United States simply walking down the streets.

But you'd never know it when looking at our media. We recently ran a cartoon in our *Levitt Letter* showing American troops attempting to demonstrate some positive aspect of their work to reporters in Iraq. The American reporters in the picture say that they're not interested in the building of schools and hospitals, the election, etc. They demand, "Just give us the body count for the day!"

In pitched battles in Iraq, typically, coalition casualties are far fewer than those of the inexperienced and more lightly armed insurgents. The insurgency is totally hopeless in terms of numbers simply because of the relative casualty figures. But our media does not report the casualties of the enemy. A typical headline might say, "Five Marines Killed in Clash," without reporting that 50 insurgents went down in the same clash. The overall picture, to be fair, is that our soldiers are overcoming the insurgents, day by day and month by month, but there are some ups and downs involved in such operations. And, of course, the virtue of the entire mission is that we are taking the fight to our enemy and not conducting it in New York and Washington.

A classic example of the media's power to distort was the almost ridiculous coverage of the abuse of the prisoners at Abu Ghraib prison. Obviously, that misbehavior should not have happened, and the Americans involved are standing trial and being punished. The American army does not advocate abusing prisoners. On the other hand, the enemy seems to get a free pass in the media for the torture, beheadings, and ongoing abuses of their own civilian prisoners. How many times have we watched horrific video of an innocent American noncombatant being held at gunpoint by a gang of masked murderers, pleading for his life? Obviously, that's part of the news, but a balance would also be pictures of, say, the substantial crowds coming out to vote. We did get some of those pictures, but nothing near the coverage of the handful of the American soldiers who got so out of line at the prison.

Another failing of the press is to mix in a healthy dose of sympathy for Muslim religious sites, often used as weapons depots or even firing positions in battles. During the fighting in Najaf, Iraq, in August 2004, the media continuously emphasized the destruction done to that "sacred" city, and drew attention to human suffering, certainly a part of any urban battle. The picture was of loutish American soldiers having a devil-may-care attitude about the religious turf and blasting innocent Muslims only trying to defend their holy sites. The fact is that there were 200+ headless bodies found in the main mosque at Najaf and hundreds of thousands of mortar, artillery, and small arms rounds. The point is hardly ever made that the Arabs scream in rage in sensitivity over their supposed holy sites, and then use those sites as military outposts or to torture people.

We related the story ("Hands Off, Please!") in our newsletter several years ago of the mosque at the University of Tulsa. According to the chief of security at an Oklahoma church, some Oral Roberts Seminary students witnessed to

Muslims near a mosque at Tulsa University. When one of
the Christians made the mistake of touching the mosque,
the Muslims insisted that his hands be cut off. Ironically,
Tulsa University built the mosque to promote diversity. This
is a typical reaction of Muslims to virtually anyone, even the
friendliest of neighbors, in defending their holy places, while
they act with such blatant *unholiness* as to undermine their
religion entirely.

It should also be noted that our media tend to stay in
enclaves of safety such as the so-called "international zone" in
downtown Baghdad. Each Iraqi city seems to have a safe haven
neighborhood, and Westerners stay close to their quarters in
those areas. However, the media are thus kept away from the
broader truth in the country and the notorious stringers come
into play if there is coverage at all outside of safe areas. Now
and then, the insurgents oblige by making some attack around
the perimeter of, for example, a hotel where Western reporters
are billeted in order to get them to report how the enemy is
"closing in." In reality, there have been next to no media casualties in these kinds of "approach" missions, but it does give our
reporters a chance to pretend that they're covering the battles
from the front lines. They're normally doing no such thing.

In Jerusalem, I have often visited the American Colony
Hotel. This nearly 100-year-old, Arab-constructed stone
building is a wonderful example of Middle Eastern archi-
tecture of the early 20th century, and it is a fine hotel. But it
caters to the citizenry of east Jerusalem, mostly "Palestinians"
who are rich enough to afford the finest in accommodations.

And it also hosts any number of American and British, etc., reporters who are immature, and imagine that they are staying in some kind of scene out of Casablanca. Indeed, the characters in the hotel, the stone archways, and the old-fashioned uniformed staff all contribute to the idea that "this is the *real* Middle East, and the Israelis are a bunch of Johnny-come-latelies who don't know how to live in the area." Never mind that the hotel is almost a stage set meant to brainwash our news people. In fact, I've heard reports that during the intifada, the hotel would actually sponsor a bus to take reporters to some upcoming "battle" between stone-throwing kids and Israeli soldiers, and the Arab powers that be would make sure the coverage was done properly. Every reporter knew that to continue his luxurious stay at the American Colony, he was obliged to file the usual kind of story, i.e., "Soldiers Attack Palestinian Villagers," or whatever.

And as to the hotel management, they were delighted to have their Western guests, who buy lots of liquor and prostitutes and promote general prosperity for the hotel and the neighborhood. That's how things really work, and those things are just not known by anyone who stays in America and reads coverage of a foreign nation.

In any case, the American and European media are two of fanatical Islam's major weapons. The Islamists manipulate the news in situations like those I've described and the media provide them a kind of prism where distortions serve the purposes of America's enemies. Generally, the focus on what successes the insurgents have damages the image of America worldwide and discourages the American public. In effect, freedom of the press has brought a growing support for the other side, and the press and the electronic media are selling lots of advertising by gathering a large audience. The old journalistic adage "If it bleeds, it leads" is being followed to the letter, and what bleeding there is in Iraq, Israel, and elsewhere is automatically featured. One would not trade this important freedom for the kind of propaganda that serves Muslim or communist societies, of course, but the price is becoming very heavy to allow cynical reporters and commentators, the Dan Rathers, Peter Jennings, Pat Buchanans, and Robert Novaks of the world, to pursue their own selfish agendas.

In this climate of misinformation and deliberate bias, it becomes even more important to know what the truth is. And I encourage you to join me in telling the truth wherever possible, not only concerning matters in our own country, but also about our sister democracy in the Middle East who stands as a solitary beacon in a sea of dictatorships. Remember, it was the Lord himself who said, "I will bless those who bless you, and I will curse him who curses you" (Gen. 12:3; NKJV).

Chapter Seven

EDUCATION —
DUMBING
DOWN

It's no secret that education has been dumbed down in the United States. Our students no longer rank very well against foreign students, and in our computer companies and scientific labs, and so on, we certainly meet a lot of what we would otherwise think of as "Third Worlders." They're smart, they've worked hard, and they have achieved something.

It puts me in mind of when I was in an *ulpan*, a language school in Jerusalem for immigrants. I was warned not to get into a class with Ethiopians. (The Israelis rescued tens of thousands of Ethiopian Jews from the poverty and backwardness of that African nation, and installed them as first-class citizens in Israel. After all, if you have a Promised Land and a Chosen

People, then all the Chosen People own that land. So much
for Zionists being racists.) I found out soon enough what the
warning was about. The Ethiopians were VERY hard workers.
If a teacher said to do five hours of homework, they would do
double that. It was very difficult to keep up with them!

In our country, political correctness, liberalism, secularism,
the emphasis on self esteem, and any number of factors have
contributed to reducing our schools to a level where our kids
just don't compete. And this has very serious consequences
for their ability to think and to understand the world around
them, especially when it comes to "controversial" issues such as
Israel's right to exist.

I have some unique qualifications to speak on this field. I
have a bachelors degree in education, and I taught, believe it
or not, students from first to ninth grades, and then in college
and even graduate school in various times in my life. I also volunteer to speak at universities on the subject of Israel to try to
correct the biased information that they're teaching about the
Holy Land. In that capacity, I have had some very interesting
encounters.

My own alma mater, Indiana University, was a big disap-
pointment for me when I was called by a Christian group on
campus to speak there in 1993. I had taken a masters degree
and all the coursework for a doctorate in Indiana. I left my
work there in 1971 when I was saved because I saw at once
that the gospel needed much more attention than finishing my
doctoral thesis, etc., so I left my studies and went to work with
Campus Crusade.

It was therefore a welcome honor for me to be asked to speak, at least to this small Christian group, at the Indiana University Student Center, and I accepted the invitation gratefully.

But there was a student in the audience whose mother was a "Palestinian" from Israel, and he gave me a hard time in the question period. I had pointed out that all archaeological evidence in Israel is Jewish and that there was no Palestinian archaeology because there simply was never a Palestinian society in Israel. There were precious few Arab archaeological discoveries of any kind because the Arabs did not tend to put up a great many buildings other than their religious shrines. They tended to move into Jewish cities that were already established when they arrived. (I was questioned by a reporter for the *IU Daily Student*, the campus newspaper, after the service. She said, "If Arabs didn't build cities, then who did build the cities they lived in?" I remember I was almost tongue-tied somehow, but what I should have said was, "Who built Bethlehem? Who built Hebron? Who built Nazareth? Are you crazy?" and walked out on her.)

I had also said that with Arab cash and Jewish brains, the Middle East could be paradise. My heckler really took offense at that, although there's no real offense to be taken. It's very clear that the Arabs, starting with the so-called Palestinians, should make immediate peace and relationships with Israel, a far superior society. There's no doubt they would profit by that relationship.

I pointed out that Israel was far stronger militarily than the so-called Palestinian society, and that I didn't see that the

Arabs would ever really win much land from the Israelis. My heckler then wrote a column about my speech in which he quoted me as saying "**** you! We've got the guns!" Of course, I had said nothing close to that, but the *Daily Student* ran his article and I was sent a clipping of it. I immediately contacted the editor and demanded equal space since my name was used and I was so badly misquoted. He agreed immediately and asked me to write an editorial of the same size. I did that and sent it in a week. I asked him for a clipping, and he agreed to send it as soon as the article ran.

The article never did run. No matter how many times I contacted that editor, and finally the faculty of the school of journalism, no one would run my article at all. I then wrote editorials in the *Levitt Letter* about this terrific attack on free speech, and I received some replies from IU alumni. That inspired me to take our ministry's mailing list and simply start with the As, sending out a letter to the effect of what had happened at Indiana University and informing the public that, as far as I could tell, my alma mater and probably many other universities had no pretensions whatsoever to "diversity" or fairness or even the doctrine of equal time and space for someone maligned in their media.

We sent out thousands of such letters! And we began to receive some wonderful answers. People who donated regularly to Indiana University cut those donations off and wrote to the university about the incident. In one case, a lawyer in Los Angeles wrote to me and said he would be glad to defend without charge a lawsuit against the university since he also was an alumnus and deeply regretted the incident. I wrote back to him, explaining my position further and that I had spoken to a Christian group. He then declared that he was Jewish, and since I was a Messianic Jew, he had thought the matter through more thoroughly and now found that, as a matter of fact, I was wrong somehow. So goes life in the Messianic side of things.

Eventually, I received a letter from Herman B. Wells, chancellor of Indiana University, who had also been in that position 20 years earlier, when I had been a student. He appealed to me to stop the letter writing and be a good alumnus. I guess the three things universities really care about are cash, cash, and cash, and he was very moved by what was happening to his donations.

I wrote back that my letter writing would stop as soon as they ran my article, but that I would not listen to any promises from the *IU Daily Student*. Once they ran my article and sent me the clipping, complete with its page and the date, I would stop the campaign.

It was inordinately difficult for the *Daily Student* to have the humility to run an editorial of an alumnus who had simply asked for equal space and had been so misquoted in the first place. But finally they wrote to me and said the article was too long for the publication, and they would run it as a letter to the editor. They would shorten it for space considerations, blah, blah, blah. I ignored them completely and continued the letter writing.

After that disappointing experience, I had no further interest at all in Indiana University or most any other college or university that I've had experience with that does not at least demonstrate some sort of fairness on an issue so important.

But that incident was only the beginning. When I did my volunteer speaking, I was called to Danville Community College in Illinois. This is a nice little school of modern buildings where some Christian people had agreed to let me come. I spoke without a fee or even travel expenses, and went to a great deal of trouble to serve that college. We drove down from Chicago (quite a distance), and had to park our trailer in a distant trailer park since Danville itself had no such facility. But I was glad to have a chance to speak to students who might have been virtually brainwashed against Israel.

But when I got to the program I noted that most of the people were of middle age. There were only the students who sponsored the engagement present, a couple of ladies, and two athletic boys in the last row staring at the ceiling as I talked. I learned later that they needed the assembly credits. They suffered through it valiantly and got their credits, but I don't think they heard a word I said. The middle-age people were from various local churches, and they enjoyed the engagement very much.

I learned later that the college had refused to publicize the event to its students. I wrote to the president of the place, and here is my letter.

Dear President Jacobs,

We received the enclosed e-mail from Ms. Conklin defending her actions on my recent speaking engagement. I direct this matter to your attention because the facts seem to indicate that she is guilty of suppressing this appearance. She would not be the first "politically correct" university administrator to give us a hard time; it's part and parcel of our daily work.

On the other hand, we deplore these tactics at a college claiming "DACC values diversity as an enhancement of those experiences in its classrooms, administrative offices, and board room. The College is committed to policies that promote fairness and inclusion for all in the life of the College. As a reflection of the College's commitment, the DACC Board of Trustees strives to promote fairness and inclusion in all policies and practices of the College."

We are holding off publishing this story until there is some settlement between these parties. My hunch is that Ms. Conklin did not like my speaking engagement, for whatever reason, and didn't do a proper job with it. At this point, she seems to be fabricating a defense; but it really isn't convincing.

President Jacobs, my wife and I hauled a trailer from Chicago to Danville and stayed overnight some 25 miles away since Danville has no adequate RV park. We served the college faithfully as we had promised, and I gave my message in full to an audience containing only two of your students. (Those, I was told, needed the assembly credits.) I did not charge a fee nor even travel expenses. It was a gift of value amounting to four figures, in our experience, to DACC, who we trusted to handle it accordingly. I'm personally very disappointed.

Could you kindly contact us at once with a credible explanation of what really happened at DACC? Thank you very much.

Sincerely,

Zola Levitt

Needless to say, we never got a satisfactory solution to the situation.

At the University of Kansas at Pittsburg, I had some Muslim hecklers. In this case, two girls who spoke with French accents but wore Muslim headdresses spoke up in the question period. I had said in my talk that I regretted that no Muslim imam had ever apologized for the World Trade Center. I had never heard a Muslim anywhere say that it was a terrible thing that happened, and that they were sorry for their co-religionists, etc. These girls insisted that there had been many apologies. I gave them my e-mail address in front of the crowd and pleaded with them to send me even just one so that I could read it and certify it. I never heard from them.

Someone in the crowd got up and accused me of being "brainwashed," and I simply asked the crowd, "Do I sound like I'm brainwashed?" And although I was preaching to the choir, so to speak, everyone including the antagonists demurred on that point. No, I did not seem brainwashed. I seemed like I had my facts. I had talked to them about Israel's right to the land. That's a talk I have given many times and the subject of an op-ed that I wrote in the *Dallas Morning News* back when they were a real newspaper and covered these sorts of issues.

Things went along in a rather bumpy way through that particular program. But suddenly, toward the end of the question period, a professor of my own age in the front row stood up and shouted, "You are the terrorist!" It's not hard to see why college students aren't getting the straight scoop on Israel and other international situations.

Just this past fall 2004, I wrote in the November *Personal Letter* about an event at SMU:

Dear Friend:

"We have shown weakness, we have not recognized the kind of enemy we are up against." So said Russian president Vladimir Putin after the massacre of children in Beslan.

We are showing weakness in our country, too. We are consistently allowing Islamic hatred and propaganda to be preached in mosques, in our government, in our courts, and especially on the campuses of our greatest universities, without penalties to these organizations.

One example was the "Palestinian Film Festival" at Southern Methodist University in Dallas in September. I have a brochure from that obnoxious exercise of "free speech."

I have some experience with this very liberal "Christian" university. When I was a beginning Campus Crusader in 1971, I attended an "Institute for Biblical Studies" on that campus. We sent missionaries to SMU's Perkins Seminary, the Methodist-operated theological school for future pastors on campus. Can you imagine? We made desperate efforts to get these United Methodists to at least come to Christ before they started their typically non-biblical ministries.

The brochure for the film festival is filled with advertising from various Muslim businesses in Dallas (which we might expect), the occasional neutral business, and finally, St. Paul Lutheran Church, a congregation of the Evangelical Lutheran Church of America. That church operates a Palestinian hospital in East Jerusalem, of which I'm all in favor.

But, several years ago, my tour was traveling to Israel on the same cruise ship as a Methodist tour group. These well-meaning church folks were all carrying packages they called "medical kits," which had been given them to take into Israel. This was most curious to me, and when we disembarked in Haifa, I mentioned the "medical kits" to the security agent as I passed through. The Methodists were behind my tour in the line, and after my group was all through, I noticed that security was requiring all of the Methodists to open their "kits." My hunch was right. Each "medical kit" actually carried some kind of contraband. I didn't really hold them responsible. The Muslims have used naïve church people forever. That tour group had a very long day getting through the Israeli security personnel.

The Muslim Legal Fund of America also took out an ad in the brochure in which they announced that they were protecting "your civil and legal rights." They pointed out that "Muslims across America have been racially profiled, have had their civil rights violated, been arrested, detained, and deported, and have seen their charities closed down by the U.S. government."

We should comment on all that: No one has their civil rights violated in America unless they are taking advantage of our democracy by promoting an alien government takeover. No one is being "profiled," except those belonging to an enemy who has attacked and killed us. I seriously doubt if anyone has been arrested, detained, and deported who wasn't really asking for it. As for Muslim charities, I think everyone knows they are a joke. These "charities" are largely nothing but front organizations sending funds directly overseas to support terrorists.

The brochure goes on to describe films about life in refugee camps. These films are all devoted to typical Palestinian propaganda; for example, how "Israeli public relations strategies exercise a powerful influence over news reporting on the Middle East conflict," as though the media favors Israel over the

Palestinians! The occasional left-wing Israeli or American Jew speaks on a panel, such as one composed of a Muslim imam, a Jewish rabbi, a Lutheran bishop, and a Presbyterian minister. Then there's a movie that claims that the "wall" (Israel's security fence) has been carefully designed to annex most of the West Bank's water and most of its good land. That is patently false. The security fence was designed to protect areas where Palestinian murderers have crossed and killed innocent civilians, and that's all there is to that. Israel has always shared its water and good land with the illegal aliens who call themselves Palestinians. At Camp David, the Israelis freely offered all the good land any people could want, but they were refused by "Chairman" Arafat who instead started a new intifada.

There's a statement called "United for Peace and Justice, a coalition of Muslims, Christians, and all other peace advocacy organizations" (as usual, no Jews invited). In a long paragraph entitled "Where Do We Stand?," the Muslims sponsoring this fiasco say that they want "to establish global peace and justice through mutual respect, peaceful cooperation, and the implementation of international law and conventions." I wonder how that applied to the World Trade Center and Pentagon attacks. The paragraph also encourages us to "end American aid and support to states that condone racism and are engaged in racist practices. . . ." We are supposed to understand by this that Israel, perhaps the most racially diverse society in the world, is racist.

That's the usual party line. (The accusation is nonsense, anyway. Israelis and Palestinians are of the same race.)

However, the crowning and most duplicitous paragraph is the following, which I quote in full:

"Palestine's long and interesting history comes alive when you visit the many archaeological sites." (In fact, there are no "Palestinian" archaeological sites in Israel. Arabs, no great builders in any case, began calling themselves "Palestinians" in 1964.) "For example, there is Jericho, the oldest town in the whole world. There is Jerusalem, Hebron, Nablus, and Gaza with their significant archaeological sites, which tell of a history that goes back thousands of years" (that would be Jewish history, of course, those all being Jewish cities from antiquity), "not forgetting Bethlehem and its biblical significance as the birthplace of Jesus Christ" (another Palestinian?).

The next-to-last page contains a remark about the "Amoud Foundation," which, as one of its activities, cites "reforestation of the region." This from the people who have again and again burned down forests as part of their terrorism against Israel.

The Palestinians simply do not deal in the truth, and we believers do. John 18:37 says, "Everyone who is of the truth hears My voice" (NKJV).

My larger point is that this war propaganda is going on in my city and yours, day after day. We did not have similar Japanese or Nazi activities going on in the United States during World War II. We looked out for it, we suppressed it, and we made sure it didn't happen. If we don't do something about the oncoming takeover on our own soil, we could lose this war. While you could not build a church or synagogue in Saudi Arabia and live to tell about it, we are nowadays seeing mosques in virtually every American city.

Of course, the United States is not alone in this world as a target for the Muslims, with all of their provocations and chicanery. The democracies of Western Europe are being overwhelmed by these noisy and indignant aggressors. It's obvious that their plan is nothing less than world domination.

All of the above is simply a sign of the end. Men are "calling good evil and evil good," and they are not dealing in the truth. How can the civilized world defeat the growing threat of a worldwide takeover by the fundamentalist Muslims?

One idea is to overwhelm them militarily, as we did with Japan and Germany. We might try to teach them to live in a democracy, as we are doing in Iraq, or we could attempt to close our borders and completely isolate ourselves, but that is not really practical either. The fact is that we can lose this war because we simply cannot subdue 20 percent of the world's population, and short of that they are going to try to convert or kill all of us.

The Western powers were able to defeat communism, Nazism, and all of the other "isms" by military force alone, but the war against terrorism is much more difficult because it's practically everywhere at once.

Modern-day political correctness is one of our major problems. We did not invite the Nazis and the Japanese emperor to participate in our country, or have receptions for their leaders in the White House or at the president's home or ranch. We acted like they were our enemies! In the United States today, liberals and Democrats are more focused on "diversity" and "tolerance" toward Muslims than they are on keeping the country safe from these people. I sometimes wonder how many American deaths it would take for them to decide that maybe we should be profiling Muslims, and keeping a real watch on them. Obviously 3,000 on 9/11 weren't enough. How about 300,000 or three million deaths? It would take but one nuclear weapon in the wrong hands to achieve such a slaughter. Would the liberals STILL be preaching tolerance and diversity toward Muslims?

The idea of teaching democracy to people who know nothing about it, in a part of the world where it has never existed, is overly optimistic. There are 25 million people in Iraq who have never experienced a

real election. They have no idea of what democracy
means. Perhaps they can have an election soon, but
what will they do when the American soldiers have
gone?

Personally, I favor instantaneous regime change for
terrorist-supporting countries such as Saudi Arabia,
Iran, and Syria. By that, I mean to go in and depose
the dictator, and then immediately ride out of town,
preferably with the dictator in irons. The argument
against this is that they will soon find a new thug to
run things and set up a similar government. We need
to let each country know that when their next government takes power, if it harbors terrorists, it will be
destroyed as well. But we must mean it and we must
really do it. It cannot be like the Vietnam War or the
lengthy community work we are currently undertak-
ing in Iraq.

When all else failed for the Israelis, targeted offense became their method of defense. In dealing with
Hamas, they first assassinated Sheik Yassin. When he
was ceremoniously replaced by Abdel Rantissi, they
killed him, too. Now, no Hamas leader wants to be
publicly recognized, but the Israelis continue, recently
killing Hamas leaders in Syria and Gaza. In addition,
they are taking out the trainers in the terrorist camps
along with those receiving the training. Aggressively
going after and killing the leaders of these terrorist
movements strikes fear into those who would follow.

The Israelis are not trying to make the Palestinians pray at the Western Wall and become good Israelis; they are not trying to promote democracy. They are simply trying to kill the terrorists before they kill more Israeli civilians. If, at times, Palestinian civilians die in the process, the Israelis are truly sorry, but that's the price of fighting against terrorism. The Palestinian terrorists, on the other hand, do everything in their power to maximize civilian casualties, particularly among women and children.

We can regard all the Muslim nations, especially Saudi Arabia, Iran, Syria, and Sudan as terrorist states and knock them down one by one. Of course, they will try to form new dictatorships, but that takes time. Let them spend their time and energy regrouping and fighting among themselves for power. That is far better than harboring and financing terrorism, as these regimes now do. If they again acquire a dictator who promotes terrorism, then we would go back and destroy his government as well, again, and again, and again, as long as it takes. And we should warn them that if any terrorism hits American shores again, then may God help them, for we will put an end to those who did that.

Obviously, I am not advocating hostilities against civilians. I mean only to take down their leaders and symbols of their governments. As with mad dogs behind a fence, we must keep these barbarians at bay.

If, at some point, they find a leader who wants to take them out of the 12th century and join the civilized world, then we might consider talking with them. But today's reality is that military force is the only thing that these terrorists really understand.

The civilized world is making the mistake of thinking that the Muslim world is made up of reasonable people. In fact, we are dealing with a so-called "religion" whose aim is to take over the world. Their plan is simple — convert all other religions to Islam and kill all who resist. There is no reasoning with people who willingly, even eagerly, throw away their very lives for the cause of Islam. In worldly terms we would call them reprobates; in Christian terms, satanic. First John 4:3 makes reference to the "spirit of the Antichrist," who we know will want to take over the world.

In order to win this war against terrorism, we should learn from Israel's fight against the Palestinians.

No one is negotiating with the Mafia, the Los Angeles gangs, or the drug dealers and trying to discover how we can help them be nicer to the rest of us. Unfortunately, we have a "War on Terrorism" like we have a "War on Drugs." These wars by our government only make the situations they are supposedly fighting even worse.

The time has come to ignore political correctness in this country and win this war. We must make a stand and pray, and, if necessary, fight with all we have.

Duke University, Berkeley, etc., are citadels of what I can only refer to as Muslim worship at a time when we have been attacked by those people. I know any number of stories I can relate about marching Palestinian students and a great deal of intimidation against the Jews. All of this, of course, is based on a phony story of Jews occupying Arab land. (See my chapter on Israel, where I address that issue.)

Berkeley has been a center of highly left-wing thinking for decades, of course. But when I visited the place, I couldn't believe how beautiful it was. I didn't speak there, but was requested to perform a wedding at that university, and went to an arboretum that overlooked San Francisco Bay from quite a distance. It was a heartbreakingly beautiful setting for a place where Jewish people are assaulted simply because they're Jewish, or, more accurately, because co-religionists of theirs who live 10,000 miles away have been accused of stealing the land they've owned for 4,000 years!

In any case, I performed a very nice Messianic wedding ceremony from notes provided by Moishe Rosen, the leader of Jews for Jesus. The bride, the groom, and guests all seemed very satisfied. There were no Muslims at the wedding and nobody standing and shouting.

I don't want to just write complaints about our school system, but rather I should make suggestions. And I have a few. First of all, we need to raise teachers' salaries in all public and private schools. Considering their importance in society, teachers should be paid like lawyers, and vice versa. If we paid better salaries, we might be able to attract better people to the teaching profession. As it is, we seem to have many people who are unqualified for anything else doing public school teaching. The last time I visited a public school was when my older boy was in high school, and I was thunderstruck by the combative and plain ignorant teacher I spoke to. I even went to the principal's office to register a complaint about her attitude, and found the principal to be a suitable comrade for her. I then gave up on public schools entirely.

When I was a public school teacher, I gave up in exasperation because of school administrators. And that would be my next suggestion. They, too, should be better paid and more educated themselves. They should be people deeply dedicated to educating students. "Professional administrators" don't make very good educators, in my view. I remember when I took my bachelors degree that the weakest faculty members in both my undergraduate and graduate schools were the education teachers. The so-called "school of education" at any university I attended was almost a joke, and the students behind the scenes were always laughing at it. My wife was a high school administrator, and a very good one. But that was a Christian school, and they seemed to care more about who was running the place than at the public schools. My younger son graduated from that school and is a powerful believing Christian today, just as is my other son.

Lastly, just like anyone else, when I read the editorial pages I deplore the idea of the weakening of standards and de facto cheating on aptitude tests. The tests must be standardized, the standards upheld, and if some students can't make the grade, that's nature. That's the human condition, and that's all there is to that. When I went to school, I had friends who went to a trade school instead of an academic high school after the eighth grade. Some remained my friends. They were good guys and gals, and they lived useful lives with the training that they undertook. We simply have to have the stomach to let some people take a different path. Some people do less academically, and some do more.

Where Christian education is concerned, we must go back to accurately teaching the Bible. Even if Moody and Dallas Seminary and the others have fallen away, it must be done in grade school and high school if we're to raise Christian people.

Private schools of all sorts are the answer, and Christian schools, of course, in particular. But they need to be properly funded. Private donations do not begin to support education. And so my thought is that everyone should support taxpayer funding of these very helpful academies which are capable of raising the best of our new citizens.

Chapter Eight

THE CHURCHES —
THE TROUBLE
WITH CHRISTIANS

I speak at a lot of churches. As of a few years ago, I began to notice that, due to our national television program, I could pretty much call churches in any given area and be accepted as a speaker by some who had members watching the program. I speak for love offerings only and for free at any university or college (in order to straighten out their Israel attitudes, if possible).

As I say when I speak, "I didn't grow up in a church. I had to get all of my information from the Bible." This sometimes gets a nervous laugh because truly few Christians do.

In my many years of speaking at churches, I have seen a steady decline in knowledge of and support for Israel. Over the

139

past three decades, our media and government have steadily turned against that small country, and in the mid-80s, the formerly scripturally sound seminaries themselves joined in. It felt to me like they were thinking, *Christianity is for nice people, and the Israelis just haven't been nice. So we have to find some doctrine to justify closing them down. We can't go as far as the replacement theology (that the Church is now Israel) that the liberal seminaries teach, but we can figure out a way to render the end times free of Israel and its influence.*

That's quite a trick, of course, in view of the fact that the Tribulation largely consists of invasions of Israel. But they tried to accomplish this sleight-of-hand with the awful doctrine called "progressive dispensationalism." This fundamental error holds that Jesus is already sitting on the throne of God, and what we have is the Kingdom itself, or at least the Kingdom coming on, and we need not concern ourselves with the details of the Tribulation — especially those awful Israelis.

Without saying it, the seminaries were simply acting in accordance with anti-Semites of every age in cutting the Chosen People and the Promised Land out of their Bible studies.

They deteriorated quite a lot. Moody began to take on professors from liberal arts colleges, and Catholic teachers, and so on, and broaden their doctrine very far. As far as prophecy went, they taught nothing that made much sense anymore. Trying to speak to a graduate of Dallas Seminary or Moody or Talbot about Israel was like bringing up some irrelevancy about some small African or Far Eastern nation. Thus, from about 1985 on, we graduated a generation of pastors utterly ignorant about the end times except to think that everything will work out well for the Church and we're at least on our way to the Kingdom, if not already there. What a silly doctrine when you look at the state of the world today.

Our seminaries have let us down in major ways. They're embarrassed by Israel for some reason, and they believe the media propaganda that it is a dangerous place and that the Israelis are brutal. Nothing could be further from the truth, but they go on willy-nilly, apparently trying to be more "mainstream." They have liberalized their doctrines in order to get more students, which brings more donations, which builds more buildings, which means that the professors, deans, provosts, etc., can ride around in luxurious cars and eat very nice lunches.

On the other hand, they have left the Lord out of it — that's the Lord who admonished, "Narrow is the way" (Matt. 7:14). If you write to Moody Bible Institute, you'll get a long, tedious, single-spaced letter protesting its undying love for Israel and its adherence to the same end-times prophecy systems as always. Former President Joseph Stowell was fond of saying that Moody had not changed its doctrine in 110 years. I have a small hope that our ministry played a small part in his early resignation. Moody's doctrine has changed from soup to nuts (and I do mean nuts). If D.L. Moody heard a talk on prophecy in that seminary today, I think he would set the place on fire (and frankly, it could use a little "fire"!).

This situation leads to pastors who graduate with a very vague grasp of "Israelology" or issues of the end times. Since the upcoming Tribulation period focuses on Israel, and since the Holy Land is God's timepiece, it certainly behooves any believer to understand prophecy and understand Israel. Unlearned pastors create unlearned church bodies who are mystified at the situation in the world today. On the other hand, a real crackerjack pastor — one who has been to Israel for more than sightseeing — has a church very alert to end-times developments and not at all surprised by the Muslim invasion, the failings of the U.N., the general decline of morality, and the "famine, and pestilences, and earthquakes in divers places" (Matt. 24:7). And they are certainly not at all bewildered by the fact that Israel is "hated of all nations" (see Matt. 24:9).

Thus, when I go out to speak, there are two kinds of churches to consider. When my staff contacts a church, they answer either, "Oh, we'd be pleased! How soon can he come?" or "Not on your life. We won't want to hear anything from Zola Levitt." (Of course, there's a namby-pamby middle ground that says, "Well, in our church we try to avoid controversy." I'm not sure if they're at all related to Jesus, Peter, and Paul, but those three did not avoid controversy, and, unlike those churches, were not striving to be the nicest people in town.)

Now, the good churches are really *very* good. They consist of what has been recently termed "Christian Zionists," but the remnant of true believers has always been Christian Zionist. Let us define Zionism: it is the wish for the Jews to return to

Israel and resettle their Promised Land. To take Him at His Word, God is a Zionist. And every right-thinking believer ought to be a Zionist.

Some time ago, the Muslims promoted an idea in the U.N. that "Zionism equals racism." They accused a country that includes and honors people of all colors, all races, all languages, from all over the world of being racist!

Anyway, the Arabs and the Jews have the same ancestor. They both descend from Abraham.

The biblical churches obviously give me warm welcome. The liberal churches are not like Christian churches at all, as far as I'm concerned. They never use Scripture, have no salvation doctrine, certainly no knowledge of Israel, and very seldom ask me to speak. And if they do, I only get a small Sunday school class, never the podium. Not in 30 years have I had the podium at any liberal denominational church. How else can they control the damage the Bible might do to their congregation?

I was once asked to speak at a large denominational church in Dallas where the potential audience was in the thousands, but the tiny group I spoke to, called the "Evangelism Committee," was only a dozen or so. After I was in the room for ten minutes, I realized no one there was saved, and so I addressed them with the Four Spiritual Laws from Campus Crusade. They weren't very happy, but I pointed out to them that they were not evangelists at all — they were just a membership committee. They went around to people's homes and tried to get them to join the church. That was for the purpose,

I gather, of getting more members, collecting more donations, building still bigger buildings, and expanding the Evangelism Committee. Frankly, I'm still not clear as to why such churches meet at all. They're basically corporations collecting and dispensing some monies to what *they* consider good causes — such as the "Palestinians."

Now, of course, when one of the big denominations divests from Israel, as the Presbyterian Church USA has done, they insult God and commit the worst of all possible errors. Saying out loud that you are not supporting the Chosen People and the Promised Land, but rather taking the side of the terrorists, is unimaginably unChristian. It simply sets a church up for judgment. Presumably, its members will be on hand to assist the Antichrist in the upcoming Tribulation.

At another instance of trying to speak at a liberal church, I was shown into a small classroom belonging to a church of some 10,000 members. A friend of mine was in the class and talked them into having me speak on end-times prophecy. I didn't know if they even knew that term, but I brought along a map and demonstrated the invasion of Gog and Magog from Ezekiel 38 and 39. I detailed how forces would come from the direction of modern Russia, as well as the satellite areas that have since become fundamentalist Muslim. I pointed out that this major event marked the beginning of the upcoming Tribulation period, a time of invasions of Israel culminating with the grand Armageddon.

I thought I had given a pretty cogent talk in the time allotted, and checked back with my friend during the ensuing week about how the class liked the presentation. He said, "Well, they thought you were a good speaker, but they couldn't make out why you were talking about either Russia or Israel in their church."

In still another case, I was invited to speak to a somewhat larger class ordinarily led by an individual who taught at a local Christian high school. My younger son had come home from a class in that school and said that the teacher told the students that "Christianity started in Greece." I took exception to that and scheduled a meeting with the headmaster of the school. The headmaster, the teacher, and I sat down together. I informed the teacher that Jesus had witnessed, as He said, "Only unto the lost sheep of the house of Israel," and that Pentecost had happened in Jerusalem. I pointed out that the gospel did not proceed to Greece until sometime later and that the mother church of Jerusalem was able to send out powerful emissaries of the Messiah to the whole Roman Empire, including Greece.

The headmaster took my side of it (thank God), and the teacher felt corrected. And so he invited me to speak to his group. They listened politely as I explained whatever information about Israel and end times seemed relevant at the time. I was thoroughly congratulated and shook many hands, but that was years ago, the church is ten blocks from my house, and I've never been asked back.

In still other instances, I'm invited to churches that surprise me (in that they really are not very biblical), but then later on the speaking engagement is suddenly canceled.

Apparently, someone in the church gets wind of the fact that I'm "controversial" or an Israel-supporter, or perhaps even just a Bible teacher.

In my book *The Trouble With Christians, The Trouble With Jews*, I wrote a chapter about the Christian condition of about ten years ago and I don't think it greatly varies today. Here are some comments I made then which are just as relevant now.

> Our style of going to church is localized, indeed. The Western church bears little resemblance to the New Testament church. We said some of that in the section on doctrine, but here we will deal with the peculiar Sunday worship service that has been adopted by trial and error in the Western world.
>
> It requires mandatory attendance like the Old Testament temple, but it should be understood that attendance was legally required at the temple because sacrifices were mandatory to atone for sin. The temple was God's dwelling place on earth ("And let them make me a sanctuary; that I may dwell among them" [Exod. 25:8]) and sacrifices were effective only at this location. It escapes most Christians that the majority of the Jewish people did not attend the temple every Sabbath — they had much less formal local synagogues for that — but they were required to go to the temple at three festival seasons per year: Passover, Pentecost, and Tabernacles.

The Western church has become so set in its ways that when the first missionaries came to Israel, they held their services at 11:00 a.m. on Sunday mornings in English. The Israelis — what few were interested — could not attend at 11:00 a.m. on Sunday because Sunday is a work day in Israel and, besides, they did not speak English. Actually, if God were at His post only at 11:00 a.m. on Sunday in the American time zones (say Virginia Beach, Tulsa, etc.), it would be Sunday evening in Israel.

As to the service itself, we have made a little pageant that we are comfortable with, but that bears no resemblance at all to New Testament worship. We have what we call a minister, or a pastor, but there is no precedent in the Bible for such a person, at least not as we have styled him: teacher, counselor, general C.E.O. of the church with his name on the sign out-side. (Nor is there a precedent for the rabbi in the Old Testament.) Our pulpit committees, stewardship and membership committees, and so forth, seem necessi-tated by our style of worship and the sheer size of our church bodies, but, again, they have no sanction in Scripture. Our seminaries differ in styles and teach-ings. To celebrate Jesus Christ, who had only one robe, Dallas Theological Seminary students must wear a suit and necktie to class every day. Those at Moody Bible Institute until recently could not wear beards, though undoubtedly the Lord and His disciples did and, in fact, the institute's founder, Rev. Dwight Moody himself, did also.

I myself made those at Moody Bible Institute uncomfortable when I spoke there since I, too, wear a beard, but I was one of Moody Press's best-selling authors and so they grimly sat through my remarks.

By and large, the church today focuses on "external" qualities in its leaders, rather than measuring their qualifications according to the specifications of the Word. The job a minister does today requires a very different set of gifts from that listed in the New Testament, as can be seen by the following:

Today's Requirements: fundraiser, dynamic personality, orator, C.E.O., administrator of staff, chair of committees

New Testament Requirements: to feed the church (Acts 20:28), oversee the flock (Acts 20:28), be an example to the believers (1 Tim. 4:12), continue in doctrine (1 Tim. 4:16), labor in the Word (1 Tim. 5:17), be able to teach (1 Tim. 3:2, 2 Tim. 2:24), be willing to work at a trade (as Paul did in Acts 18).

The minister of today is considered a fine minister indeed if he is a great orator. A compelling style of speech-making seems to take precedence over knowledge of Scripture. The requirements we have today for a pastor are practically the same as those for any corporate executive. Although these skills can certainly be useful to a minister of God, it is the inner spiritual gifts and the attitude of the heart that are of paramount importance.

Music is also important in most churches, as indeed it was in biblical worship. But there is an enormous variety in the approach of individual churches and denominations to the music they use in their services, from decorous congregations using symphonies, to charismatics with a full brass band accompanying a type of spiritual hoedown, to the Church of Christ with no instruments allowed at all. And these are all reading the same New Testament.

The 300-year-old music used in many churches is peculiar. We play no Bach or other serious Christian music, in general, other than ancient hymns that are well below the musical understanding of even the adults in the modern audience. The music is very dated and, if the truth is told, sometimes unscriptural. J.B. Phillips, in his book *Your God Is Too Small*, lists some hymn phrases that are misleading, if not outright distorted. Verses such as "Gentle Jesus, meek and mild/ Look upon a little child" and "Christian children all must be/ Mild, obedient, good as He" conjure up a picture of a timid Jesus, someone who might have trouble working up enough anger to whip the money-changers out of the temple. Others seem to imply that faith is a form of escapism, as in "Hide me, O my Savior, hide/ Till the storm of life be past/ Safe into the haven guide/ O receive my soul at last." And there is almost a sort of holy masochism in "Oh to be nothing, nothing/ Only to lie at His feet/ A broken and emptied vessel/ For the Master's use made meet [fitting]."

Choirs today barely read music in churches where they could be singing the magnificent cantatas of J.S. Bach Sunday after Sunday and learning a new one for each service (at the speedy rate at which the master composed them)! We are more likely now, in the larger churches, to hire professional musicians, unbelievers or whomever, to perform the more difficult pieces like Handel's Messiah, which congregations once sang on their own. As a young oboe player, before I came to Christ, I was glad to have Easter or Christmas "gigs" in churches. They paid well, the audience was not overly discriminating, and the music was relatively straightforward and simple. The only difficulty church jobs presented to the musicians of the time was that it was difficult to sneak a cigarette, since there were no intermissions.

The idea of bringing unbelieving musicians to the church brings to mind an unusual but relevant Old Testament prohibition:

> And as for the perfume which thou shalt make, ye shall not make to yourselves according

to the composition thereof: it shall be unto thee holy for the LORD. Whosoever shall make like unto that, to smell thereto, shall even be cut off from his people (Exod. 30:37–38).

God gave specific instructions for the making of the incense to be used in worship, and issued a dire warning against anyone making a synthetic type, "like unto that" of the real incense. An important prohibition is given concerning worship: no "strange" incense is to be offered. This speaks of simulated or purely formal worship.

What seems to be meant is that the worship wafting up to God ("the perfume") should not be artificially created. Praise to God through music must involve hearts that have been made "holy for the Lord." Bringing in unbelievers to add worldly talent to Christian worship is simply unholy. It is just one more way that the church has gotten off track because Christians do not know the Scripture, which is the foundation of our faith and therefore should be the foundation of our practice.

And so the church in America, which should be the most ardent supporter of the land of our Lord, instead has focused its eyes on the world and has adapted itself to the world's way of thinking. Except for the remnant of true believers, its members are by and large ignorant of Scripture and content to remain so, and its pastors are more concerned with running a business than feeding the flock. The church needs a wake-up call and soon, but I fear that the call will be the Rapture followed by the Tribulation, and that it will catch most Christians napping.

Chapter Nine

THE END TIMES — FROM HERE TO ETERNITY

In the chapter on our government I laid out one possible scenario for the unfolding of the Tribulation, which Scripture promises will be a terrible time. All indications are that it will be soon. There are wars and rumors of wars, leaders who call evil good, and mounting natural disasters. The recent tsunami in Asia seems to be part of end-times prophecy. Our Lord warned of "famines, and pestilences, and earthquakes, in divers places" (Matt. 24:7) and it seems He sent them all in a single day.

There has been so much news about this incredible disaster that I don't have to fill in the facts in this space. Suffice it to say, however, that the tsunami is not alone in a pattern of increasing natural catastrophes.

There were amazingly strong hurricanes, four consecutive ones, in Florida the previous fall. There were horrific rains and mudslides in California almost simultaneous with the tsunami. Terrible snowstorms wracked the Midwest and even south Texas! Folks in San Antonio drove south toward the Mexican border so their kids could build snowmen and throw snowballs! The northern states suffered through a particularly bitter and difficult winter.

This is not to mention overseas calamities of the same sort. Either they are increasing in number and fury, or perhaps we're just getting more dramatic media reports. But in any case, our Lord's observation seems more than justified for our time.

Another theological aspect of the great tidal wave in the Indian Ocean was the Muslim theories of blame-fixing. Some imams preached that Israel, America, and India, in some combination, were testing nuclear weapons and caused the disaster. Others said it was Allah who wanted to kill 200 Americans and didn't mind losing nearly a quarter of a million Muslims along with them. Still others said those who perished had it coming since they went to those beaches for play and fornication anyhow, instead of maintaining their proper religious chastity.

The Islamic thinkers outdid each other, as usual, in sounding utterly ridiculous.

After a U.N. official described the first American reaction as "stingy," there came a kind of donating contest where different-size countries anted up different amounts for aid to the victims. The United States led the pack because, in addition to its usual government funds and sending troops to aid survivors, private contributors all over America gladly pitched in to help out. This was striking in view of the fact that they were helping hostile Muslim areas where the United States is known as the Great Satan, and where they burn the flag and shout "Death to America" as a matter of course. Indonesia, one of the world's really backward Muslim societies, was hardest hit in the storm.

Indonesia reluctantly accepted the help of the United States and Israel, which was utterly crucial to the survival of thousands, but still gave back the usual insults and derision. This was sort of like a primitive tribe insulting the most advanced societies in the world and, in fact, that was sort of what happened.

Israel instantly volunteered to send its expert teams of doctors and field hospitals, which helped Muslims in Turkey and Bosnia, but the help was rejected by most nations simply because they were Jewish. Behind the scenes, Israel continued to send aid as it was allowed, and, as always, was a major contributor. (Israel also took in boat people from the same area of the world back in the '70s. These refugees from the Vietnam war were turned away or accepted by various nations, and Israel, very experienced at bringing in refugees, gladly extended a helping hand. As matters now stand, they enjoy wonderful cooking in Vietnamese restaurants throughout the land because of their kindness. I assume when the refugees alighted on Israel's shores they were asked what they could do, and they said, "We can cook." I have eaten in those restaurants, and they were telling the truth.)

If the unbeliever had only a modicum of end-times knowledge — if the Israelis, for example, who will be the objective of all end-times hostility, would just read the prophecies in the Bible that their ancestors wrote and published — there wouldn't be much confusion about what is happening. If prophecy teachers are correct, and I join most of them in their estimations, the Tribulation Period with its starvation, disease, and natural calamities, is very close indeed. To make it more convincing, the Lord said in Matthew 24:8: "All these are the beginning of sorrows," with reference to labor pains.

No one ever ignores labor. No one puts a woman in labor to bed and covers her up and says, "You'll feel better in the morning." While there is such a thing as false labor, everyone takes the pains that precede a delivery seriously. In an amazing case at Presbyterian Hospital in Dallas, I was told that a woman arrived for 19 consecutive nights experiencing false labor. On the 20th night, she delivered a perfectly normal baby. The moral of the story is that on all the previous nights everyone suited up, set up a delivery room and took her perfectly seriously. No one said, "Oh, let's go home. She's never going to have a baby."

We should likewise take very seriously the signs of the end which match our Lord's prophecy perfectly. The only thing perhaps lacking is intensity, and no one can say how many storms equal a Tribulation Period. But a word to the wise would be to take these disasters as seriously as we would take advanced labor pains.

We have explained the events of end-times prophecy as far as the unbeliever goes — the Tribulation Period, the Antichrist, etc. — but not the outcome of the end times for the believers. I was surprised to learn, as I began to speak in churches, that the study of prophecy seemed less important to people than other elements of the New Testament. The liberal churches don't bother with it at all, and even in the biblical churches, the knowledge is hazy. There are arguments about whether the Rapture might occur before, during, or after the Tribulation Period, and there are discussions about the world heading toward Armageddon. Apart from that, there are virtually no details about what happens to us in heaven, and what we do when we get back here to earth, and to the Kingdom.

Back when Israel was first re-established in 1948, the seminaries played a big role in encouraging the study of the end times because it seemed apparent that God was preparing to work out the rest of the Tribulation. The Tribulation, after all, is basically an international assault on the Jews in Israel, and the necessity of them being back in the land caused good Bible students to think about the end. Dallas Seminary, Moody Bible Institute, Talbot Seminary, etc., led the charge to pay close attention to what the prophets said about the "end of days" and "the day of the Lord."

Professor Dwight Pentecost of DTS put out a wonderful book called *Things to Come* that was a rather thorough and complex analysis of the end times. Hal Lindsey followed up with the very popular *The Late Great Planet Earth*, one of the best-selling books of the entire 20th century. It varied from

Pentecost's scholarly work by being accessible to lay readers — a kind of prophetic *Reader's Digest*. The book was very
accurate and discussed the most complex biblical forecasts in
everyday words. Some 35 million people very much enjoyed it.

Dr. McCall of our ministry and I followed up in the early
'70s with our *Satan in the Sanctuary* about the oncoming
Tribulation temple, and *The Coming Russian Invasion of Israel*
about the invasion of Gog and Magog, and we continued to
put out books on the Rapture, etc., taking one prophecy at a
time and explaining it thoroughly in popular language.

Those books were all best sellers, and every publisher
wanted to put out something new on the end times.

But the enemy was working full-time against us, and after
the 1973 war in Israel, the Arabs promoted an embargo of oil
that had Americans waiting in line to gas up their cars. The
propaganda was that the Israelis were so awful that they made
Arabs do bad things. The media took their side of it, invariably
being rather anti-Semitic to begin with, and pretty soon tiny
Israel became painted as the bad guy. Imagine calling a nation
of some six million people a formidable foe of 350 million
Arabs! While they outnumbered the "Palestinians" in the land,
they certainly extended them every kindness, at least back
then. Until the Palestinians began to engage in serious terrorism and the murder of innocent people, the Israelis gave them
every accommodation. It is not an exaggeration to say that the
Palestinians, even today among the best-off of any Arabs in the
Middle East, could have prospered greatly by simply partici-
pating in Israel's democracy, but they did not cooperate.

As a result, prophecy is becoming the unmentionable biblical subject among churches and with Christian publishers these days, and of course that is ironic at just the time that so much of it is coming to pass.

Many believers are apparently unaware of the true nature of most publishers that put out Christian books. I addressed this subject in our February 2004 *Levitt Letter*, "A Note from Zola."

Dear Friends:

I received the following thought-provoking letter and couldn't help but pour my heart out in my reply.

Dear Zola,

Last year my husband gave me a New King James *Open Bible* by Thomas Nelson Publishing. It was a wonderful Bible; that is, until I started looking at the maps and reading the notes. Israel is more often than not referred to as "Palestine." This really upset me so I called their Customer Service line and shared my extreme dissatisfaction with the fact that they called Israel "Palestine." I told her that nowhere in the Bible is Israel called Palestine and that I thought it heretical that Thomas Nelson would do this.

She gave me some lame-brained excuse about the historical usage of the name. So, I hung up and wrote them an e-mail. I got an even worse excuse. I could no longer stand to use that Bible (a very expensive one) and I gave it away.

This afternoon, a friend of mine brought me a copy of your newsletter and I was so happy to read your "A Note From Zola" which addresses in depth this problem of Bible notes. Kudos to you. Meanwhile, I am telling everyone (including Thomas Nelson) that I will no longer buy any of their publications — including Bibles — until they remedy this problem.

Here is my answer: Of course the problem with Thomas Nelson is that, like Zondervan, it is run by (to a large degree) secular businessmen, who only want to make money. I am not surprised that their biblical sensitivity has greatly declined. I had trouble with them when I authored one book for them years ago. Likewise with Zondervan, who objected when our ministry questioned their publication of the awful *A Survey of the New Testament*, by Robert H. Gundry, which was used at the Criswell College.

Unfortunately, Christians often sell their companies to the highest bidder when they retire, and then that new owner damages the faith while helping himself to Christian funds.

That goes right along with Revelation 2:9, in regard to "the blasphemy of those who say they are Jews and are not, but are a synagogue of Satan." This passage, often misunderstood, refers to unbelievers who had infiltrated the highly Jewish church of Smyrna and dressed as Jews to appear as legitimate members of the church, while their real motive was simply to trade with the church members for their own gains.

When I was in college, I applied for a job with Metropolitan Life Insurance Company. I was asked if I would be available to go to church every Sunday. I informed my interviewer that I was Jewish and had never been in a church, to which he replied something like, "Don't worry about that, we don't go for any other purpose but to sell insurance to church members."

So in regard to unbelievers who take over or infiltrate Christian congregations (as with many liberal churches), with perverse Catholic priests, with Hollywood personalities making religious movies, and finally with these mediocre publishers, we simply have to watch out for what Scripture calls, "false prophets, which come to you in sheep's clothing, but inwardly they are ravening wolves" (Matt. 7:15).

Time and again we hear from folks who object to the *Levitt Letter* dealing with "politics." It is really not politics we are trying to comment on, but rather prophecy apparently being fulfilled. The biblical picture of the end times projects a certain configuration of nations and powers, and we are in a ministry of comparing the actions of those nations to the observations of the prophets. Far more of our readers are heartened by the similarities between events today and Scripture than are offended by this coverage.

Please know that we do consider this type of commentary to be Bible teaching. The real problem is that many seminaries and churches have been remiss in not preparing believers for real application of the biblical end-times scenarios. They just don't teach accurate prophecy. As watchmen "for the house of Israel" (Ezek. 33:7), we must sound whatever alarms we perceive to be relevant.

We have detailed in an earlier chapter the failings of various churches to understand this important doctrine and to appreciate that Israel is the unfortunate target of the Tribulation Period. But the question arises whether Bible prophecy is still valid!

It doesn't seem like a reasonable question, but Tyndale House Publishers, originally the purveyors of *The Living Bible* and other very doctrinally accurate works of Christian literature, are now going to publish a book on the preterist viewpoint. This strange rendition of Bible prophecy claims that it all happened back in the first century. As to where we are now on the prophetic calendar, it's anybody's guess. If this is the Kingdom, we must be very disappointed. If it's eternity, why are people dying and why are there so many unbelievers around? And if it's neither one, what happens to Revelation, Isaiah, Daniel, and all those other books about the end times — Jeremiah, Ezekiel, Zechariah, etc.? Voluminous sections of the Bible have to be disregarded to uphold this doctrine.

But my point is, a reputable Christian publisher through whom this author released some of his early books, has gone for the money in this case, it would appear. They published Tim LaHaye's superb *Left Behind* series, and now they are going to release the opposite point of view. Their defense, like that of all venal publishing houses, is that a broad spectrum of ideas is needed to understand the subject.

That is reminiscent of Notre Dame, Columbia, Berkeley, and other universities that insist on having the most rabid Muslim fanatics on the faculty in order to participate in "the marketplace of ideas." Our young people are taught utter propaganda in the name of "diversity" and "open minds." When I speak on college campuses, I am almost run out of town on a rail for insisting that the concept of the Chosen People and the Promised Land is not only still valid but obviously leading us in a very biblical direction these days.

Zondervan publishes the error-prone *Survey of the New Testament* by Robert H. Gundry, and Moody, Dallas, and Talbot Seminaries, have gone in a bizarre direction with that doctrine called "progressive dispensationalism," which, in a word, involves the disenfranchisement of Israel and the muddying of all the end-times prophetic knowledge. (See the author's *Battles with Seminaries*, written with Dr. Thomas S. McCall, senior theologian of Zola Levitt Ministries, for details on "discussions" with these misguided seminarians.)

Bible prophecy is still valid. It's more valid today than it was a week ago and a month ago. It is evidently so relevant that those who understand it are on the edge of their seats in today's exciting world. It appears that the day of the Lord is dawning and the end times are on their way. The Antichrist is waiting for his cue.

And at a time like this, when so many have turned away!

But, in a way, it seems as though the pendulum might be swinging back. At the Pre-Tribulation Conference in Dallas in December 2004, several professors, including the president of Dallas Seminary, presented a very pro-Israel commentary. The conference itself devoted its entire agenda to Israel, and, while that may have made some of those more liberal seminarians a bit uncomfortable, the truth rang out from all sides.

But it's one thing to get them to realize that the unbelievers' Tribulation Period is on its way, and they should be sensitive to that — especially in testifying of Christ — and quite another thing to get them to teach the real destiny of the believers. It seems crazy to say the churchmen don't know how to advise the church on where it's going, but I'm afraid that's exactly what I have to say.

And so, now I'll discuss where the Church is really heading. I think I can do that best by sharing from my very successful little booklet *Glory: The Future of the Believers*.

I. Glory!

Somehow, when we study prophecy in the Church, we seem to focus most of our attention on the future of the unbelievers. The oncoming Tribulation period, the actions of the Antichrist, and Armageddon are explained over and over again as if they were the main concerns of the believing Church.

This interest in the Tribulation period is natural, of course, since the approach of this culmination of God's plan also signals the approach of the return of our Lord. But it is a much happier subject, and of much greater concern to the believers, for us to look at the future of those who will go to heaven during the Tribulation period and then return with the Lord to populate the Kingdom on earth. After all, the prime difference between the biblical faith and worldly religions is that with Christ we have a bright future. What we see is not all we get. The life in this world is of little importance to those who have been promised the Kingdom to come. We are already living our eternal lives, of course, and this is the worst part of them.

So let's look beyond — beginning with the Rapture of the Church – and see what will happen to each one of us who has believed in the Lord Jesus Christ and helped carry His cross in this life.

II. The Rapture

The prime questions that come up about the Rapture of the Church are 1) What is it?, and 2) When is it?

As to question one, of course, the Rapture of the church describes the moment when the Lord will come and take the believers with Him to heaven. This is the great promise of Christianity and the great difference between that biblical faith and the common worldly religions. Buddha will not be making another appearance, and Mohammed has not promised to return for his followers. The various cults that come and go normally last only for a season, sometimes only as long as their original founder exists on the earth. But the followers of Christ rest assured of a great deliverance to come, a true deliverance of the Chosen People to the Promised Land.

It is sad that there are Christian churches which have not disclosed the doctrine of the Rapture of the Church to their members. The liberal churches which have put the Bible away have thus lost the prime promise of Jesus Christ, and live on in a pathetic "Christian ethic" — a meaningless and powerless copy of what they think the life in Christ might be. The believers who understand the Rapture and await the coming of the King, on the other hand, live in a new Kingdom in an ongoing eternal life.

The word Rapture is borrowed from the Latin Vulgate Bible, and appears in the English Bible as "caught up," in 1 Thessalonians 4:17. The final three verses of 1 Thessalonians 4 contain the prime promise of the return of the Lord for the Church:

> For the Lord himself shall descend from heaven with a shout, with the voice of the archangel, and with the trump of God: and the dead in Christ shall rise first: Then we which are alive and remain shall be caught up together with them in the clouds, to meet the Lord in the air: and so shall we ever be with the Lord. Wherefore comfort one another with these words (1 Thess. 4:16–18).

Verse 18 above is not quoted as much as the others, but it certainly should be. What is more comforting than to think that we will go beyond this life and then "ever be with the Lord"?

The Lord first indicated that He would be departing from the Church and then returning again on His final Passover night. In that nerve-racking scene in the upper room He gave His disciples the momentous message:

> Let not your heart be troubled: ye believe in God, believe also in me. In my Father's house are many mansions: if it were not so, I would have told you. I go to prepare a place

for you. And if I go and prepare a place for you, I will come again, and receive you unto myself; that were I am, there ye may be also (John 14:1–3).

After His resurrection and the 40 days with the disciples, in which He taught them "the things pertaining to the kingdom of God" (Acts 1:3), the Lord rose to His Father, and the promise of His return was repeated:

> And when he had spoken these things, while they beheld, he was taken up; and a cloud received him out of their sight. And while they looked steadfastly toward heaven as he went up, behold, two men stood by them in white apparel: Which also said, Ye men of Galilee, why stand ye gazing up into heaven? This same Jesus, which is taken up from you into heaven, shall so come in like manner as ye have seen him go into heaven (Acts 1:9–11).

It is interesting that the Lord, having only 40 days left with the Church, thought to teach them not so much how to behave, but the things of the Kingdom to come. His final messages were about the Kingdom and about witnessing to all men:

> But ye shall receive power, after that the
> Holy Ghost is come upon you: and ye shall
> be witnesses unto me both in Jerusalem, and
> in all Judea, and in Samaria, and unto the ut-
> termost part of the earth (Acts 1:8).

The two men in white apparel were angels, of course, who had come to reassure the disciples that in just the manner they had seen the Lord ascend — that is upward toward heaven — He would return. They would someday see Him come back from the clouds of heaven.

Thus the Lord is not to return "in a spiritual way" or "within your human heart," but literally in the manner that He left. Precisely, He will descend from heaven. In that the Lord thought to spend His last moments on earth explaining the things of the Kingdom to the church, we should in like manner concentrate on those things of the Kingdom to come, and this is my reason for writing this book. The Rapture, of course, is only the beginning. We will continue on to the things of the Kingdom below.

We gain additional information about the Rapture from Paul's first letter to the Corinthians:

> For as in Adam all die, even so in Christ
> shall all be made alive. But every man in his
> own order: Christ the firstfruits; afterward

they that are Christ's at his coming (1 Cor. 15:22–23).

The Scripture says that every man born of Adam, every human being, dies, but those in Christ will be resurrected. It also indicates that we have an order ("every man in his own order"). This ties in with "the dead in Christ will rise first." Jesus is called the first fruits since He is the first man permanently resurrected. First fruits is the proper name of the third Jewish feast, Resurrection Sunday, which we have come to call Easter. If we refer to it as First Fruits, then we realize that there is a second, a third, and so on. In point of fact, we all have a number, and we will rise in that order in the Rapture of the church. Naturally, the dead in Christ will rise first since they obviously have lower numbers. Jesus' number was one. Let us hope that by the time of the arrival of the Lord the numbers will go into the billions!

The most interesting facet of the Rapture of the Church is that each believer will undergo a mysterious metamorphosis: we will be changed in a way that will outfit us for eternal life. The bodies we have now will not be good for that; most of them are barely good enough for this earthly life:

Behold, I shew you a mystery; We shall not all sleep, but we shall all be changed. In a moment, in the twinkling of an eye, at the last trump: for the trumpet shall sound, and the dead shall be raised incorruptible, and we shall be changed. For this corruptible must put on incorruption, and this mortal must put on immortality (1 Corinthians 15:51–53).

Death is the common fear of all mortal beings, and every human being stands in fear of it — except the true believer. Paul exults in the face of death:

O death, where is thy sting? O grave, where is thy victory? The sting of death is sin; and the strength of sin is the law. But thanks be to God, which giveth us the victory through our Lord Jesus Christ (1 Cor. 15:55–57).

Once the Rapture of the Church is accomplished, then we are ready for the exciting events of our seven years in heaven while the Tribulation period takes place on the earth below.

The Rapture is more fully covered in the books, *Raptured*, and *The Signs of the End — The Millennium*, both co-authored by Dr. Thomas S. McCall and myself.

III. In Heaven

Once the believers arrive in heaven with the Lord, we have important matters to transact. We are not issued wings and harps, but instead we have a serious conference with the Lord, aimed at preparing us for our wedding. We are, at this time, the bride of Christ; in heaven, we shall become the wife of the Lord.

The first event is a kind of review of our life of service for the Lord while on earth:

> For we must all appear before the judg-
> ment seat of Christ; that every one may
> receive the things done in his body, according
> to that he hath done, whether it be good or
> bad (2 Cor. 5:10).

It would appear that each of us meets individually and privately with the Lord at this "judgment seat" in order to evaluate with Him our lives on earth. The emphasis is not on our sins, of course, which were forgiven long ago at the Cross, but on our works. The believer is saved "unto good works" and, of course, has a responsibility as a disciple of Christ. If it were not that we were appointed to certain tasks on earth — as workers in a field, soldiers in the spiritual battle, and so on — we could all have gone to heaven the moment we were saved. As it is, we have accomplished, or failed to accomplish, certain assignments given us according to our gifts.

Paul expounds quite specifically on the standards in the judgment seat of Christ, and how our works are to be reckoned:

> For other foundation can no man lay than that is laid, which is Jesus Christ. Now if any man build upon this foundation gold, silver, precious stones, wood, hay, stubble; Every man's work shall be made manifest: for the day shall declare it, because it shall be revealed by fire; and the fire shall try every man's work of what sort it is (1 Cor. 3:11–13).

Paul first establishes that no foundation for this life can be laid outside of that in Jesus Christ. Good works done outside of Christ — those done by unbelievers — do not come into this Scripture, because, of course, the unbelievers will not be going to heaven. What good works, and sins, the unbelievers accumulate in this life will be presented at the Great White Throne of judgment after the Kingdom.

After Paul establishes that the believer has laid his foundation in Christ, he now divides the work into two categories, calling them "gold, silver, and precious stones," on the one hand, and "wood, hay, and stubble" on the other. Obviously, those are two very different rankings of quality. The Lord will try all of our works with fire.

The image is very clear, since fire will certainly show the difference between the gold, silver, and precious stones works and those of wood, hay, and stubble. The precious metals and stones would not be harmed by fire, but the wood, hay, and stubble will all be burned away, and that is the purpose of the judgment seat.

Obviously, each believer has a life of great variety to present to the Lord, and we cannot always be sure ourselves just which works of ours are considered of high value in heaven, and which are worth not more than those flammable materials. We recall in the gospel the story of the man who prayed and fasted so much and thanked God that he was not of the class of the poor beggar who lay on his face at the back of the synagogue. The beggar, at the same time, was only pleading, "Have mercy on me, a sinner." As the Lord explained the story, it was found that the beggar's humility and pleas for mercy were the real gold, silver, and precious stones, and all of the holy protests of the supposedly righteous one in the front were the worthless hypocrisy of wood, hay, and stubble.

Paul now specifies that we shall be rewarded for the works that survive the fire:

> If any man's work abide which he hath
> built thereupon, he shall receive a reward (1
> Cor. 3:14).

We shall receive jewels for our crowns for the good works we have done in this life. It is well to remember that the rewards of the Christian come at the end of this life in heaven and not on this earth.

Paul also specifies that we shall suffer loss for the works that do not qualify — the wood, hay, and stubble:

> If any man's work shall be burned, he shall
> suffer loss: but he himself shall be saved; yet so
> as by fire (1 Cor. 3:15).

We must notice in the passage above the phrase "but he himself shall be saved." God is very clear on the point that salvation is a free gift, not an earned prize. We cannot lose our salvation by bad works, and certainly not by sins, which were forgiven the moment we came to belief in Christ. We shall suffer loss of our rewards, in effect, for our bad works, but we shall not fall back out of heaven. Peter thought the heavy net of fish which he had "caught up" might break, and some fish might fall back into the water (John 21:11). However, the Lord had selected the fish on this occasion, and none were lost once they were caught up.

The fire, of course, is not meant to consume the believer. God has fire that does not burn, such as with the burning bush and the lake of fire. The fire is only to purify away the bad works, as fire sterilizes away bacteria from foods. The sense of the judgment seat of Christ is to prepare us as a spotless bride for the Lord (2 Cor. 11:2). If we were to go on to our wedding with the Lord with the consciousness that our sins are forgiven, but with the memory of many bad works we had done in lifetimes of service, we would have, as it were, a guilty conscience, and we would not be the pure virgins the Lord wishes as His bride. Thus, the judgment seat of Christ is the final preparation for the marriage supper of the Lamb. Just as an earthly bride adorns herself in her finest garments, so we will go before the Lord cleansed of all bad works, forgiven of all sins, and in effect, as perfect as He is himself.

It sometimes surprises many believers, in their humility, that we will indeed be the equal of Christ in purity, in the future. But this is our destiny; the Scripture is very clear. Christ could not marry less a bride than He himself is, and of course, we shall reign with Him in the Kingdom as the queen on the earth.

This, then, is true Christianity, a transcendence of this worldly life, this worldly state, this worldly body, this worldly mind, and this entire worldly labor — we trade it all for a state of eternal bliss in the presence of God himself in Christ Jesus.

IV. The Marriage

Now we are ready to marry the Lord.

It is fascinating to compare the events in heaven
with the wedding tradition of Israel in the time of
Christ. There was a seven-day "honeymoon" in the
bridal chamber for the bride and groom, preceding
the reception or marriage supper. This pertains exactly
to the seven years in heaven and the judgment seat
of Christ, leading up to the marriage with Him. The
Jewish wedding and all of its Gospel implications are
explained fully in another book of this series, *A Christian Love Story*.

John covers the marriage scene for us in two glorious verses in his Revelation of Jesus Christ:

> Let us be glad and rejoice, and give hon-
> our to him: for the marriage of the Lamb is
> come, and his wife hath made herself ready.
> And to her was granted that she should be
> arrayed in fine linen, clean and white: for the
> fine linen is the righteousness of saints (Rev.
> 19:7–8).

The white linen costumes, or bridal gowns, that
we shall wear when we marry the Lamb fulfill a fascinating Bible type that reaches back to the tabernacle of
ancient Israel (Exod. 25–30). In the tabernacle, plain
white linen was associated with pure righteousness.

The linen curtains around the entire tabernacle, the tent, as it were, were pure white. No one could enter through the sides or the rear because they would have to have been perfectly righteous to pass through the white linen. The door of the tabernacle, however, was sewn with the colors of Christ — scarlet, purple and blue threads, indicating sacrifice, royalty, and heaven. All the Israelites had to enter by the door and, of course, the implication was that they were entering by means of the Messiah. Jesus said, "I am the door: by me if any man enter in, he shall be saved, and shall go in and out, and find pasture" (John 10:9). The priests of the tabernacle were obliged to wear the Messianic colors in their costumes, and the colors also appeared in the hangings of the various courts and on the coverings that made up the roof.

But now, the Church shall wear white! "Fine linen, clean and white, for the fine linen is the righteousness of saints." The very fact that we can now appear in white — glowing white, as it were, as did Christ after His resurrection — testifies to our final perfection.

Paul compared earthly marriage to this great marriage of Christ and the Church (Eph. 5:21–33). In heaven, we will see the final fulfillment of the apostles' patient exhortation of the infant Church.

When our marriage to the Lord is accomplished in heaven, we will be ready to immediately return

to earth with Him to occupy His kingdom. This is
exactly the manner in which, in the Israeli wedding,
the bride returned with her bridegroom after the
marriage to housing he had arranged for them. They
did not remain in his father's house, but instead
departed for their own abode.

V. The Return

The return of the Lord to the earth is given in glorious terms in the Scriptures. John's writing becomes
breathtaking:

> And I saw heaven opened, and behold a
> white horse; and he that sat upon him was
> called Faithful and True, and in righteous-
> ness he doth judge and make war. His eyes
> were as a flame of fire, and on his head were
> many crowns, and he had a name written,
> that no man knew, but he himself. And he
> was clothed with a vesture dipped in blood:
> and his name is called The Word of God. And
> the armies which were in heaven followed
> him upon white horses, clothed in fine linen,
> white and clean. And out of his mouth goeth
> a sharp sword, that with it he should smite
> the nations; and he shall rule them with a rod
> of iron: and he treadeth the winepress of the
> fierceness and wrath of Almighty God. And

he hath on his vesture and his thigh a name
written, KING OF KINGS, AND LORD OF
LORDS (Rev.19:11–16).

It is the Church that is viewed in verse 14 above.
We temporarily come as an army in order to put a
stop to the battle of Armageddon, which will be in
progress on earth at the moment we return.

Once Armageddon is taken care of, we shall see
the judgment of those who lived during the Tribulation period, and the rewarding of those who refused
to receive the mark of the Antichrist, but instead were
martyred for their faith in Christ:

> And I saw thrones, and they sat upon
> them, and judgment was given unto them:
> and I saw the souls of them that were behead-
> ed for the witness of Jesus, and for the word
> of God, and which had not worshipped the
> beast, neither his image, neither had received
> his mark upon their foreheads, or in their
> hands; and they lived and reigned with Christ
> a thousand years (Rev. 20:4).

The unbelievers, however, will be bound 1,000
years, until the final judgment:

But the rest of the dead lived not again
until the thousand years were finished. This is
the first resurrection (Rev.20:5).

John exults over the fact that we are blessed to take
part in this first resurrection and to reign with Christ
through the Kingdom Age:

Blessed and holy is he that hath part in
the first resurrection: on such the second
death hath no power, but they shall be priests
of God and of Christ, and shall reign with
him a thousand years (Rev. 20:6).

More details were given by the Lord during His
earthly ministry about this judgment, which serves as
an immigration office into the Kingdom. He means
to take care of every single soul who existed during
the seven years on earth, when the Tribulation period
was in progress. The Lord is so perfectly fair. All of the
nations will be gathered before Him, and He will separate the believers from the unbelievers "as a shepherd
divideth his sheep from the goats":

When the Son of man shall come in his
glory, and all the holy angels with him, then
shall he sit upon the throne of his glory: And

before him shall be gathered all nations: and
he shall separate them one from another, as a
shepherd divideth his sheep from the goats:
And he shall set the sheep on his right hand,
but the goats on the left. Then shall the King
say unto them on his right hand, Come, ye
blessed of my Father, inherit the kingdom
prepared for you from the foundation of the
world (Matt.25:31–34).

In reply, the believers will express surprise that they
had so honored the Lord during the Tribulation period, but He will make the matter very clear to them:

And the King shall answer and say unto
them, Verily I say unto you, Inasmuch as ye
have done it unto one of the least of these
my brethren, ye have done it unto me (Matt.
25:40).

If the people of the nations of the world, even
during the Tribulation period, demonstrate faith in
Christ by caring for his brethren (the 144,000 of Israel
who witness during that hard time), they will be saved.
But the judgment is equal and devastating upon
those who failed to honor the Lord during the reign of
the Antichrist:

Then shall he answer them, saying, Verily I say unto you, Inasmuch as ye did it not
to one of the least of these, ye did it not to
me. And these shall go away into everlasting
punishment: but the righteous into life eternal
(Matt. 25:45–46).

The Old Testament saints will be regathered as
well at the beginning of the Kingdom Age, and so
the Kingdom will get under way with rather a mixed
crowd, all having in common a sincere belief in the
Messiah and King. There will be the faithful of the
Old Testament, who waited so long for this grand
age, the believers of the Church Age, who went to
heaven in the Rapture, and finally the believers of
the Tribulation period, who will enter the Kingdom
in their natural bodies. Since they did not come to
faith before the Rapture, they were not changed and
they remain as they are, still marrying and giving in
marriage, unlike the believers of the Church Age. This
latter group, the people in their natural bodies, will
give birth during the Kingdom to ordinary, fleshly
sinners, again "born of Adam." It is these few on
earth, in the Kingdom, who will occasionally disobey
the Lord's commands and make it necessary for Him
to set penalties for failures of worship or sanctity (e.g.,
Zech. 14:16–19).

These mischief makers in the Kingdom, having multiplied, will be rallied by Satan in the very last battle at the end of the thousand years:

> And when the thousand years are expired,
> Satan shall be loosed out of his prison. And
> shall go out to deceive the nations which are
> in the four quarters of the earth, Gog and
> Magog, to gather them together to battle: the
> number of whom is as the sand of the sea.
> And they went up on the breadth of the earth,
> and compassed the camp of the saints about,
> and the beloved city: and fire came down from
> God out of heaven, and devoured them (Rev.
> 20:7–9).

This last rebellion of Satan is unsuccessful and the Great White Throne of judgment is set up for all those who were confined with him, and the unbelievers of all ages:

> And I saw a great white throne, and him
> that sat on it, from whose face the earth and
> the heaven fled away; and there was found
> no place for them. And I saw the dead, small
> and great, stand before God; and the books
> were opened: and another book was opened,
> which is the book of life: and the dead were

judged out of those things which were written
in the books, according to their works. And
the sea gave up the dead which were in it; and
death and hell delivered up the dead which
were in them: and they were judged every
man according to their works. And death and
hell were cast into the lake of fire. This is the
second death. And whosoever was not found
written in the book of life was cast into the
lake of fire (Rev. 20:11–15).

This second death, then, is that which is avoided
by the believers in Christ.

VI. The Kingdom

Of course, there are a thousand great years between our return from heaven with the Lord and
that throne of judgment for the unbelievers. And this
Kingdom Age, this great millennium, is the true reward of the Church. We should go back and examine
it.

The Kingdom will be quite a different age than
we have now. Things will be socially "upside-down."
It will be sophisticated to be a Christian then, and
downright foolish to be an unbeliever. The King himself shall reign in Jerusalem with us, the queen.

We must turn to the Old Testament for knowledge of the Kingdom, since that's where Jesus got His

teaching. There was no New Testament, of course, at the time the Lord taught the disciples "the things pertaining to the Kingdom" (Acts 1:3), but the great passages of Isaiah and the other prophets make clear this magnificent age of God's triumph. The New Testament assumed that everyone understood the Kingdom, since it had been already explained in the Old, and it virtually began with the Sermon on the Mount — the explanation of how one gets into the Kingdom and how the law of the Kingdom will be. The Beatitudes (Matt. 5, etc.) continue to inspire us as to that idyllic age of God's total sovereignty over the earth.

Isaiah's passages ring with beauty:

> But with righteousness shall he judge the poor, and reprove with equity for the meek of the earth: and he shall smite the earth with the rod of his mouth, and with the breath of his lips shall he slap the wicked. And righteousness shall be the girdle of his loins, and faithfulness the girdle of his reins. The wolf also shall dwell with the lamb, and the leopard shall lie down with the kid; and the calf and the young lion and the fatling together; and a little child shall lead them. And the cow and the bear shall feed; their young ones shall lie down together: and the lion shall eat straw like

the ox and the sucking child shall play on the
hole of the asp, and the weaned child shall put
his hand on the cockatrice' den. They shall not
hurt nor destroy in all my holy mountain: for
the earth shall be full of the knowledge of the
Lord, as the waters cover the sea (Isa. 11:4–9).

Nowhere in the Bible is the Kingdom more con-
cisely and more beautifully described than in Isaiah's
very brief chapter 12. We quote it in full:

And in that day thou shalt say, Oh Lord,
I will praise thee: though thou wast angry
with me, thine anger is turned away, and thou
comfortedst me. Behold, God is my salvation;
I will trust, and not be afraid: for the Lord
Jehovah is my strength and my song; he also is
become my salvation. Therefore with joy shall
ye draw water out of the wells of salvations,
and in that day shall ye say, Praise the Lord,
call upon his name, declare his doings among
the people, make mention that his name is
exalted. Sing unto the Lord; for he hath done
excellent things: this is known in all the earth.
Cry out and shout, thou inhabitant of Zion:
for great is the Holy One of Israel in the midst
of thee.

Isaiah 9:6–7 will be fully realized ("Unto us a child is born. . .").

We could go on and on in the other prophets with the marvelous descriptions of life on earth in the presence of the King. The theme of it will be the constant company of Jesus, the total triumph of the saints, and absolute justice and mercy throughout all the earth. This, again, is the reward of the true Church.

VII. Eternity

After the Kingdom and the White Throne of judgment, we are still not finished. The believers go on in the mysterious period known as eternity, about which little can be said since the Scriptures are very cryptic. God is going to change heaven, earth, and Jerusalem — there will be no more seas — no more water and therefore no more life as we now know it. However, we shall continue to live on with the Lord in eternity under those strange new circumstances.

The biblical writing becomes symbolic, almost incomprehensible, at the very end of the Scriptures as John describes his revelation. We can sample the description of eternity as John saw it and wrote it for us in Revelation 21:

> And I saw a new heaven and a new earth:
> for the first heaven and the first earth were
> passed away; and there was no more sea. And I

John saw the holy city, new Jerusalem, coming
down from God out of heaven, prepared as a
bride adorned for her husband. And I heard a
great voice out of heaven saying, Behold, the
tabernacle of God is with men, and he will
dwell with them, and they shall be his people,
and God himself shall be with them, and be
their God. And God shall wipe away all tears
from their eyes; and there shall be no more
death, neither sorrow, nor crying, neither
shall there be any more pain: for the former
things are passed away. And he that sat upon
the throne said, Behold, I make all things
new. And he said unto me, Write: for these
words are true and faithful. And he said unto
me, It is done. I am Alpha and Omega, the
beginning and the end. I will give unto him
that is athirst of the fountain of the water of
life freely. He that overcometh shall inherit all
things; and I will be his God, and he shall be
my son (Rev. 21:1–7).

One notable feature is that eternity will not have a
temple:

And I saw no temple therein: for the Lord
God Almighty and the Lamb are the temple
of it (Rev. 21:22).

We might surmise that no temple is needed because there certainly need be no further sacrifice, and, in effect, no further worship. Everyone who then exists will be one with God, or so closely in touch with God that there would be no point to them having to contact Him through the medium of a temple. The implication of the Scripture is that God Almighty and the Lamb may be approached directly in eternity.

Another interesting feature is that there will be a new kind of light. Light was virtually the first thing God made in creation, but now there will be no further need of the sun nor the moon because God and the Lamb provide all the light:

> And the city had no need of the sun, neither of the moon, to shine in it: for the glory of God did lighten it, and the Lamb is the light thereof (Rev. 21:23).

The most striking feature of eternity is that there will be not even a whisper of evil about it. While there was a certain amount of rebellion in the Kingdom, as we saw above, eternity will be utterly free of "anything that defileth":

> And they shall bring the glory and honour of the nations into it. And there shall be in

no wise enter into it any thing that defilers,
neither whatsoever workers abomination, or
maketh a lie: but they which are written in the
Lamb's book of life (Rev. 21:26–27).

And remember, this is only the beginning!

John, after seeing all these things, made the most
logical conclusion, and one that all Christians might
make. The thing to do, he felt, was to pray immediately for the soon coming of our Lord Jesus Christ. John
the Apostle, a New Testament saint, a member of the
Church, awaited the Rapture fervently — as fervently
as we ought to. The conclusion of the Bible is more
than a fitting conclusion for this discussion. John's
final prayer must be our ultimate prayer. In view of
all he had seen in this stunning Revelation of Jesus
Christ, John uttered simply:

He which testifieth these things saith,
Surely I come quickly. Amen. Even so, come,
Lord Jesus. The grace of our Lord Jesus Christ
be with you all. Amen (Rev. 22:20–21).

CHAPTER Ten

QUESTIONS AND ANSWERS — THE HEART OF THE MATTER

Before I was on television I had a radio talk show called *The Heart of the Matter*. It started rather small, but ended up attracting a very large Christian listenership who asked a great many Bible questions, both of the guests I had on the program and on open-line shows.

I really didn't know a great deal of Scripture back then, and I stayed pretty close to Dr. Thomas McCall, my friend and mentor, and now the senior theologian of Zola Levitt Ministries. In general, the people tended to ask the same questions again and again, and I got pretty good at those answers. Now and again, someone would surprise me and I'd ask for a day to think it over, and I'd check with Tom.

In any case, there follow in this chapter the most popular questions, those that repeated again and again, and seemed to very much interest at least the Christians of the Dallas-Fort Worth metroplex, and, by extension, probably Bible people everywhere.

Q. *Can you lose your salvation?*

A. I actually "lost my salvation" four different times while broadcasting that radio program. The first was occasioned when my guest was Dr. Vernon McGee, the respected radio Bible teacher, who shocked me when he asserted that he didn't feel that modern Israel was a fulfillment of prophecy. In view of the fact that my ministry focuses on exactly the opposite, I disagreed with him, and we went into a bit of a struggle, with Dr. McGee doing almost all the talking so that I couldn't ask many questions. I would have brought up the dry bones vision (Ezek. 37), of course, and other seeming indications that what we have now in Israel at least leads to the end times, but he was having none of it. By the end of the program, I don't think he was enjoying the visit.

But what ensued next amazed me. A group wrote in to say that they were "praying for my salvation." I didn't understand that you could lose your salvation by disagreeing with Dr. McGee!

On another occasion, the Church of Christ took my salvation away because I disclosed that I played the organ at a local Hebrew Christian mission (what they now call a Messianic congregation; I pastor one myself these days).

The United Pentecostals took it away one day by questioning my baptism. It was in the Jordan River, but the formula that Tom pronounced over me was "In the name of the Father, the Son, and the Holy Spirit," and these people insisted that I had to be baptized "in Jesus' name," and that's all.

A lady called in about my baptism, taking me step by step after her incredulous question, "Mr. Levitt, were *you* baptized?" I told her I was. She asked if it was in a Baptist Church. I specified that it was in the Jordan River. There was a long pause and, not to be outdone, she said, "Well, was it by a Baptist minister?" And, as a matter of fact, my friend Tom is an ordained Baptist minister, as am I, so I could answer her positively. She seemed disappointed, but satisfied.

I also "lost my salvation" by having a homosexual on my radio program. His name had been used on the station and he asked for equal time, which used to be the doctrine on the radio. (These days you can say anything about anybody and they don't get a chance to retort.)

And so, the Rev. Jerry Sloan, pastor of a "gay church," and his lesbian assistant pastor came to the program. I asked them in a pre-interview if they were practicing homosexuals, and Rev. Sloan said, "Well, I think we've got it down pat."

Naturally, I took exception to Sloan's attitude about his sin, but I was not condemning. I can't say that for the audience, however. They vied with each other in remonstrating with this sinner in a manner that did not make me proud. I remember going to one commercial break by saying, "I'll be back with the Rev. Jerry Sloan for more of his stoning right after this."

It wasn't exactly that I took some strong position one way or another, but I tried always to be an accommodating host, whomever my guest might be, though, of course, I didn't agree with all of them. That didn't stop a lady from calling a few days later on an open-line program and asking, "Mr. Levitt, are *you* a homosexual?" I told her, "Look, I understand why you ask me that and, as a matter of fact, you did not hit one of my sins with your guess. But let me assure you, I *am* a sinner, and I'm not in a position to condemn sinners. Our Lord never condemned a sinner."

That started up quite a discussion about sin and forgiveness, etc., which I think was all to the good.

Finally, a lady called in and said, "Well, I'm not a sinner. I don't have any sins at all." I could not help pointing out to her that 1 John 1:8 says, "If we say that we have no sin, we deceive ourselves, and the truth is not in us." I told her, "You're at a minimum a liar." After that discussion, more folks started praying for my salvation.

What's the answer to the question? I think no, you cannot lose your salvation. It's the free gift of God. You can abuse a gift. You can even throw a gift away. But it was given, you received it, and in this case God said, "I will remember their sin no more." The transaction is done, and you are a party to it. No matter how you twist and turn, you will not get away from our Lord, who said, "No one shall pluck them from my father's hand" (John 10:28). I know there are arguments to the contrary, but they usually are emotionally based. Everyone knows someone who is so very sinful indeed they contend that he must have lost his salvation. But, usually, when I sit and talk out such cases in detail, we come to the point where the individual in question probably never was saved to begin with, or has simply backslidden, a familiar and forgivable situation.

I know it's quite an argument, but I'll stay with eternal salvation. Sin is forgivable, other than the sin of blasphemy of the Holy Spirit, which I take to be in this day and age a common unbelief in the Lord as Savior.

Now on to more questions.

Q. *How do we get three days and three nights from the crucifixion to the resurrection if the Lord was buried on Friday and came out of the tomb on Sunday morning?*

A. The answer to that has to do with how days are counted in Jewish tradition. Each day is regarded as starting at sundown and continuing until sundown the next evening. Thus, if the Lord were crucified on Friday, that day would have started on Thursday night. (The concept is not unknown in the Western world. If you have an invitation to a New Year's party, you know to go to it not on January 1, which really is the New Year, but on the eve of December 31. Likewise with the Christmas Eve worship, etc.)

Another example would be if a male child is born late on an afternoon, he is regarded as having already experienced one night and one day for purposes of circumcision. The eighth day is counted from the eve before the day of his birth. Thus, if the child were born before sundown on June 1, his circumcision would be planned for the daytime of June 8, even though by Western reckoning that's only seven days.

Since the Lord's crucifixion and burial occurred during Friday's daylight hours, what we would call Thursday night was included. And that counted as a night and a day. Then it follows that He was in the tomb Friday night, and that was His second night. Saturday daytime was His second day. Saturday night was the third night. And Sunday, since He was resurrected in daytime ("after the sunrise"), is the third day.

This concept is peculiar to the Western mind and yet that is the way it is counted in Israel. A convincing piece of evidence would be that Palm Sunday occurred during that week. Exodus 12:4 tells us that before the Passover lamb was to be sacrificed, people were to observe it for four days to be sure that it was without blemish, was healthy, etc. (God did not want the people sacrificing sick or otherwise blemished animals.) Since the Lord came down the Mount of Olives on a Sunday, then four days from then would necessarily take us to the following Thursday. On that night, the Passover Seder was held and the Lord ate His last supper.

Reasoning based on the day of unleavened bread being called a Sabbath that week tend to ruin the Sunday to Sunday schedule clearly announced in the Gospels. It is also a most convincing demonstration of the victorious Friday crucifixion that the day was, from then on, referred to as Good Friday.

Q. The next most popular question would probably be: *"When was the Sabbath changed to Sunday?"*

A. That never happened. If one wishes to honor the Sabbath, then it is Saturday. Sunday is the Lord's Day, the day of His resurrection, the day when the churches meet, and always a Christian worship time. In the New Testament, the Sabbath is not a requirement (see Col. 2:16–17).

Actually, keeping the Sabbath instead of worshiping on Sunday, as some denominations do, is a different question. Whether kept or not, the Sabbath is always Saturday, the seventh day of the week, on which God rested. I can't resist telling a tale that happened in Ithaca, New York. I actually traced it there and it was verified for me there. It seemed that a drugstore across the street from a church was serving a delicious new confection known as an ice cream soda, and the young people in the church were so eager to drink these delicious sodas that they rushed out of church and sometimes even left early.

The deacons of the church talked about that problem and decided to approach the druggist and tell him that soda water was intoxicating and should not be served. The druggist, a qualified pharmacist, told them that was silly, but if it would accommodate the church, he would omit the soda water and simply serve a scoop of ice cream with the syrup on it. And he would call that new confection a "soda for Sunday."

The deacons lived with this for a while, but realized that the young people simply referred to this marvelous new offering as a "Sunday," and so they approached the druggist again, telling him that he could not name a mere confection after the Sabbath, or so they put it.

The druggist negotiated again and they settled with his changing the spelling of the name of the new confection, and that is how we got the ice cream "sundae."

Sabbath-keeping is a troubling and divisive issue in the Church, and yet Scripture is clear on it not being a necessity. After all, the true meaning of the Sabbath was a day of rest, and the Lord himself said, "*I* will give you rest" (Matt. 11:28, emphasis added). Keeping any feature of the Old Covenant with a view toward pleasing God amounts to overlooking the fact that He has made a New Covenant (Jer. 31:31–34; Heb. 8:8–12). In a sense, it takes a bit of the Law and brings it up into the age of grace. Or put another way, if one wishes to keep *some* Law, then one puts oneself under *all* the laws in order to be consistent. That would not befit the Christian Church.

Q. Probably the next most frequent question is about the timing of the Rapture: *Is the Rapture before, during, or after the Tribulation Period (or is there going to be a Rapture at all)?*

A. I come down strongly for the pre-Tribulation setting for the Rapture, and without going into theological tangles, I have a very simple reason. The Rapture is a surprise. The Lord described it as happening "in the twinkling of an eye," or "like lightning across the sky," and thus, we are surprised when it happens. It's not that we don't expect it some day, but we simply don't know the moment. In a parallel example, the bride of Israel, whose prospective groom had departed to build her a mansion, a bridal chamber at his father's house, was certainly going to return for her, but she simply did not know when. She waited for him every night.

If the Rapture is to surprise us, then it certainly can't follow any obvious event that we all can see. If, for example, the Rapture were at the end of the Tribulation period, as is taught in some circles, well then I could watch the events unfold, check my calendar, and be packed and ready when the Lord would come. In fact, He would come on the 2520th day after the Antichrist signs his covenant with Israel, that being seven biblical years for the Tribulation period. I would be able to verify my calculations by watching the Antichrist blaspheme in the temple at 1,260 days, the midpoint (see Matt. 24:15 and 2 Thess. 2:3–4). Obviously, the surprise would be gone and we would not be talking about the Rapture described by our Lord.

Verses like Revelation 3:10 and 1 Thessalonians 1–5 also clearly describe a pre-Tribulation Rapture, along with others. But I have always found in debating the point with folks who hold other positions, that their arguments have an emotional quality rather than sticking to Scripture. In other words, they may say, "The Church has been full of sin and evil and ought to be punished. God is angry and we deserve His wrath." That just isn't scripturally so. The Church itself is a haven for sinners and that's well known. And salvation in its most intensive sense means that our sins are forgiven and forgotten in this Covenant when it comes to the Resurrection.

Q. *What will we do when we get to heaven?*

A. I have a booklet on this subject called *In My Father's House*, and it describes the interesting activities that lay before all believers after the Rapture. The first thing we will do in heaven is stand before the judgment seat of Christ (2 Cor. 5:10). This judgment is about the works we have done with the gifts we have. All Christians are gifted in many ways, and are charged with certain duties by the Lord in this life. (Otherwise, we could presumably go right on to heaven the moment we're saved.) The details of this judgment are given in 1 Corinthians 3:11–15, where we see our works done in this life divided into gold, silver, and precious stones on the one hand, and wood, hay, and stubble on the other. The Lord tries all the works with a fire and the negative works are burned away. The precious metals and jewels are not harmed by the fire, and we are thus "purified." At that moment, we really are "perfect." Our sins were forgiven at the Cross, and now our bad works are done away with, and we are a fit bride to literally marry the Lord.

And that's the next piece of good news. We then proceed to our wedding. Revelation 19:7–8 tells us that we don white wedding gowns, and have a real marriage supper with the Lord. The Judgment Seat was the honeymoon — the honeymoon is where the groom removes the veils of the bride and knows her secrets, and it's the place where we confront the Lord with all that we have done — and the marriage supper is what we would call the wedding reception. At that point, we are outfitted to be the queen of the Kingdom to come, and we will proceed on to that happy duty next.

Q. *Another question that often comes up when I teach is about the identity of the 144,000 witnesses during the Tribulation, even though that is given clearly in Scripture.*

A. Revelation 7:4 gives us the number, and the ensuing verses tell us that 12,000 come from each of the 12 tribes of Israel. They're obviously Jewish people who are saved as if by an electric current through the nation when they are needed (when the Church is absent because of the pre-Tribulation Rapture). When God chooses witnesses, He always chooses Jews, as in Genesis 11 when the Tower of Babel is built. At the end of that chapter we read of Tera and the birth of Abraham, the choice of the Jewish people. And Christ's disciples and apostles were all Jews. Finally, these 144,000 Jews will serve the Lord in the same capacity, testifying of Christ in the world when there's no other testimony available.

I'm sometimes asked if I will be one of them, and I answer, "No, I'm going in the Rapture with you!" In reality, Jews that we witness to here, who are not saved, seem to be likely candidates to be in that select group to do that important Tribulation period work. But we'll know more when the time comes.

Jehovah's Witnesses, some Mormons, etc., make a claim on the 144,000, but this simply requires ignoring the letter of Scripture and is a fanciful expansion of cultic thinking.

Q. *A question I was asked more in the past than recently concerns the red heifer. Some people believe that the next temple, which will exist at the time of the Tribulation, cannot be built unless the ashes of a purely red heifer are available to purify it. Dr. McCall, the senior theologian of our ministry, refers to it as the red herring, and that's what I think it really is.*

A. The way I heard the original story was from an Orthodox Jewish friend in Jerusalem who reported that the man who started it didn't really mean to, and that the ashes of the red heifer were never found. It seems that archaeologists were digging at the temple site, and this good, black-suited, very devout Orthodox Jew became offended, thinking of how many people were buried in the area, concerned over the fact that they might dig into a grave or touch bones with their tools, or whatever, which would be a desecration, a terrible desecration in Judaism. As he watched, he began to imagine that they could even strike the ashes of the red heifer, and that's what he said to a different "black suit" standing by. That one, in turn, turned to a group and said, "We think they've struck the ashes of the red heifer." And they each turned around and told others, and on it went.

Needless to say, the story traveled like wildfire through the Orthodox community of Jerusalem, and in an hour probably everyone had heard it. The dig was stopped (that was the original intent of the observers and something they do all the time). The archaeologist assured the multitudes that no such thing had happened, and it was extremely implausible that it ever would. And they, being experts at digging ancient ruins, doubted very much that they would strike upon ashes that were 2,000 years old, and so on. But nothing would quiet the story.

But that was nothing in comparison to what happened when it hit the Christian Church, and began to travel from town to town in the United States. People could talk of almost nothing else. Ranchers everywhere began to raise cattle to try to get a red heifer. From time to time, someone would summon a rabbi to examine an animal, and the rabbi would, sure enough, find four little white hairs with his magnifying glass and disqualify it.

Several points need to be noted here. First, it didn't really happen. Second, if they found some kind of box with some kind of ashes and could somehow verify that these were the very ashes of the red heifer, it wouldn't be a very important find. After all, the second temple survived without even the ark of the covenant. The ashes of the red heifer were used in an obscure ceremony to purify a priest who had walked through a graveyard. (Muslims are buried in front of the east gate of the temple in order to impede the entrance of the Jewish King, whom they think cannot walk through their graves. Apart from other considerations, the Jewish king is not a priest of Levi, but of the tribe of Judah, and is well aware that His way will be impeded. I'm not worried.)

The temple can be built and the worship go on as always, with or without those ashes. But it brings up the third point, which is what I call the "ministry of distraction." People come along and seem to distract the Church from its real purposes — witness and good works, charity and so on — and fascinate folks with stories like these. The "finding" of the ark of the covenant, of Noah's ark, etc., goes on and on, and people will invest themselves heart and soul into such projects, and lay awake at night thinking about them. But that is not the business of the Church on earth. It simply distracts us.

I can name the stories that have come down the road over the years of similar irrelevance as the red heifer. There were the vultures laying more eggs for the Russian invasion in order to clean up the bodies; there were social security cards with alleged numbers 666 on them; the United States is supposedly sending stones from a quarry in Bedford, Indiana, to build the third temple; and the list goes on. (I went to Indiana University near Bedford. It is built of wonderful limestone, and the temple would look splendid with Indiana limestone. But the fact is that Israel has loads of such stones and always has had. In any case, nobody ships a thousand-ton stone 10,000 miles to build anything!)

You could probably add a few more from your own experience of these sensational stories. There are ministries out there purporting to teach prophecy that come up with such novel items and write reams of doctrine about them and, again, distract the church. But they serve no useful purpose.

There are stories going around that "the Rapture is limited to only good Christians," or people of a given denomination, or people who are prepared in some way with a correct baptism and an excellent testimony, etc. To me, the Rapture is simply the removal of the converted sinners. It's not necessarily for good people. It's for everyone who has come to faith in Jesus Christ for remission of sins. As to good Christians, I don't know who they are.

Q. *Can Jewish people be saved by keeping their Law?*

A. Here and there, one runs into what's called the "dual covenant," where Jews are saved by the Law and Christians by their faith. This is totally invalid. If Jews could be saved by their Law, then Jesus chose the one country where He could completely waste His time. The Jewish Law required sacrifices and other external performances as demonstrations of faith in the Messiah to come. Romans 3:25 tells of God being patient with an unregenerate people as long as they properly demonstrated their faith, until the coming of Messiah. Then, in effect, the Messiah would review their files and grant the salvation where people demonstrated faith. Whether in the Old Covenant or the New, faith is the requirement for salvation. We never get it by works, we never earn it, and we never merit salvation as a reward for good behavior.

We once ran a cartoon in the *Levitt Letter* showing a bunch of Jewish sages addressing the Lord himself and saying, "We get our salvation the old fashioned way: we earn it!" Believers should know what the Lord might have answered to that one.

Q. *Do the Arabs come from Ishmael in the same sense that the Jews come from Isaac?*

A. Many try to say that the so-called "Palestinians" have a right to land in Israel since their forebear Ishmael was also a son of Abraham. But the Jews descend from Isaac through a system allowing no intermarriage and are therefore always one family. Jews have married converts to Judaism, but they break the Law if they marry outside of the faith. Descendants of Ishmael, however, went in all directions among an enormously varied population of Middle Eastern people. Ishmael himself, for example, went down into Egypt and married an Egyptian woman, as the record states. What his descendants did from that point is unrecorded.

There is no Arabic law corresponding to the Jewish laws against intermarriage. Descendants of Ishmael married willy-nilly where they pleased and created an enormous culture of different tribes and languages.

It should be said that, even if they did, God cleared it up in Genesis 17:20–21 where He says to Abraham, ". . . as for Ishmael, I have heard thee: Behold, I have blessed him, and will make him fruitful and will multiply him exceedingly; twelve princes shall he beget, and I will make him a great nation. *But my covenant will I establish with Isaac*" [emphasis added]. The Jewish people, and only they, descended from Abraham through Isaac, Jacob, and the 12 tribes, have ownership of the land of Israel.

Q. *Is it safe to travel to Israel?*

A. Israel is one of the safest countries in the world, unless you watch CNN or read the *New York Times*, etc. I have almost belabored the point on my television program and in our newsletters that Israel has so far fewer casualties than the

United States that it would be taking a break from almost any American community to visit the Holy Land.

Rather than asking if it's safe to travel in Israel, we should ask where the travel warnings are for Washington, DC? And where's the international peace conference for the United States, which murders some 16,000 people per year in peacetime? The country of Israel, much smaller, of course, is still incomparably safer. Less than 1,000 people have died in terrorist actions during the present four-year intifadah.

Q. *I've been asked to support oil exploration in Israel. Is that a hopeful investment?*

A. Many people inspired by various scriptural verses have tried to find oil in Israel, to no avail. A few years ago, someone looked at a map and decided that if, as Jacob prophesied in Genesis 49 "Asher shall dip his foot in oil," then the lower portion of Asher's territories near Caesarea should yield oil.

It is olive well that is referred to in Scripture. Asher was appreciated for its contribution of excellent olive oil for use in the Jerusalem temple. The Scripture does not ever refer to petroleum.

Nevertheless, a well was drilled that went down more than 20,000 feet and was completely dry. Similar results have happened from other such events. Typically, these projects raise a great deal of money and expend it as they're supposed to. But nowhere in prophecy is it indicated that Israel will achieve any significant riches before the Kingdom comes.

Q. *Should I give to American charities that support Israel?*

A. I give to various charities bringing Jews out of Russia and other places, helping them to emigrate to Israel. That is a worthy cause, and if the money is given to Christian people, it is normally well used. But charity for Israel should be sent to Israel. Sending such monies to American middlemen is gambling. Some of them are very ethical and do the right thing. Others, unbelievers of various sorts, are open to question on how much of the charity is kept for administrative fees in America, etc.

Our ministry has three simple questions that you may ask of any such charity when you give, and that includes unbelievers' charities as well. Will you provide a financial statement, what percentage of my gift will actually go to the recipient, and will you provide the name and e-mail address of the recipient so I may verify that my gift arrived safely? If you can't get positive results with those three questions, don't give to that charity.

Q. *Will the Jews really flee to Petra when the Antichrist blasphemes in the temple?*

A. The verse referred to is Matthew 24:15, etc., where the Lord advises those who are in Judea to flee into the hills. It is thought by many teachers that they will go all the way to Petra in southern Jordan to avoid the Antichrist and his regime. Isaiah 34 and Isaiah 63 both mention Bozrah, thought to be local reference to Petra, as a place where the Lord stops and battles evil forces, apparently at the Second Coming. In both scenes, He comes out with His robes dripping red, and the thinking is that He has rescued His brethren, the Jews who fled to that hiding place. He then would proceed to the Mount of Olives, and the Jews there in Jerusalem would "look upon Him whom they have pierced and mourn for Him as for an only son, a fount of cleansing will open unto the House of David" (Zech. 12:10; 13:1).

Q. *Many times, when I'm speaking, the question arises, "Is the United States mentioned in end-times prophecy?"*

A. The fact is, our country is not mentioned for several reasons. We're too far from God's theater of operations to make much difference in the cataclysmic end times. All of that, of course, will take place around Israel, and is, in fact, a series of attempted invasions of the land, culminating with Armageddon. Secondly, we will not be a world power at that time due to the fact that the Rapture of the Church will "lift off" the better portion of America, which is to say, its right-thinking and moral citizens.

We all realize that there are two Americas. Part of the United States is moral, upright, democratic, free, and wishing the best to everyone, especially the Promised Land. A second America is found outside of any biblical or moral issues, and that is a country of crime, drugs, pornography, terrific violence, and so forth.

It is hardly appreciated that our country has far more crime than any of our peers. It is also not appreciated that almost anywhere in America is far more dangerous than in Israel or in any European nation. In some ways, we have the best and the worst of everything, and that is to be expected in a very large, very free democracy. But the Rapture will separate "the sheep from the goats," as it were, and the remaining Americans will probably join in a NATO-like alliance with the Antichrist and end up attacking Israel in that cataclysmic final battle.

Many teachers have tried to find snippets of Scripture to justify including our country in the end times. Many of our seminaries erroneously teach that God has withdrawn His hand from Israel and placed it upon America. We imagine, that because we send many missionaries, and have many churches, that we are now some kind of new "chosen people." All of this is a local conceit. God's story is thousands of years in the making, and the end times, like all the times before them, will concern Israel and how the nations have dealt with it. I sympathize with those teachers and students who want to give our great country a prominent place in the plan of God, but I cannot honestly say that I find it anywhere in end-times prophecy.

Q. *Where is the ark of the covenant?*

A. The ark is most likely hidden underground on the Temple Mount. Israel was besieged by Nebuchadnezzar and the Chaldeans at the time they hid it away, and it would have been very difficult for them to leave the temple platform.

Stories about it being in Pisgah, Jordan, or even Ethiopia, are fanciful yarns on a par with Indiana Jones stories. One would have to accept not only a romance, but a marriage of

King Solomon and the Queen of Sheba, that they had children, and their descendants somehow spirited the ark all the way from Jerusalem across the Sinai to some hiding place in her kingdom.

The ark, it must be appreciated, was a sizable chunk of solid gold of inestimable value to a hundred marauding tribes who frequented the vast desert flats of Sinai.

The Arab Muslims apparently believe this too, since they have placed their Temple Mount shrine right on the platform apparently to keep the Jews from excavating for this one-of-a-kind find.

Q. *Who is the Antichrist and is he alive today?*

A. He must be alive and mature, and probably already pursuing a successful career in geopolitics. In view of the nearness of the end, according to all prophetic signs, the Antichrist is like an actor waiting offstage for his cue to step into the drama and play his part.

People make guesses based on different characteristics of various leaders. Through the ages they have selected certain popes, Napoleon, Stalin, Hitler, etc. More recently they've chosen Nelson Rockefeller, who was rich and powerful, Reverend Moon of the "Moonies," and Bill Clinton. (In the last case, the specification of Daniel 11:37 that he will "not regard the desire for women" would require some reforming.)

The Antichrist will be revealed after the Rapture, I believe, and it is information we can only continue to guess at. In a peculiar way, I suppose the individual does not even realize that he is groomed to become the right hand of God's enemy in an upcoming globalized world. If he doesn't know himself, we can't know him either.

Q. *Do the Arabs have a biblical claim to land in Israel?*

A. No. Ancestral land in Israel belongs to the Jews, according to God, who gave it to them. They are "the indigenous people of the Holy Land." The ancestral lands of all Arabs are in Arabia.

Q. *How were you saved?*

A. By reading Scripture.